Praise for *Rivers and Ice*

"Breathtaking—a flipped raft snarled in a snag while two paddlers barely make it to shore. Breathtaking—a goshawk diving straight at the eyes of two women hikers diving flat into mud. Breathtaking—a woman crying in the American Cemetery in Florence Italy as she recognizes for the first time the risks and sacrifices her troubled father made so she could live. Susan Pope brings alive these moments and so many more in her deeply moving evocations of five generations of lives well lived in an ever-changing Alaska. A book of marvels, breathtaking."

Peggy Shumaker, former Alaska Writer Laureate, and author of *Just Breathe Normally* and *Cairn*

"Candid, quiet, and clear-eyed, *Rivers and Ice* is a richly authentic memoir by a nearly lifelong Alaskan, best appreciated by the reader who has little patience for overromanticized portraits of the 49th state—a tribute to fragile places, imperfect love, the allure and cost of adventure, and the challenges of family legacies."

Andromeda Romano-Lax, author of *The Deepest Lake*, and *Annie and the Wolves*

"With unflinching honesty, Susan Pope explores the complexities of a uniquely Alaskan life's journey that will resonate with readers no matter where they live. Vacillating between frozen and flowing, the human and geographic landscapes she explores are hauntingly beautiful and complex. A memorable exploration of resilience and hope that gives readers much to ponder."

Deb Vanasse, author of *Wealth Woman* and *Roar of the Sea*

"*Rivers and Ice* is lovely, full of heart and humility, courage and kindness. From the prologue, which immediately immerses us into Alaska's wilderness, to Pope's page-turner memoir of growing up in the Anchorage of the 1950s, it flows with the braided grace of an Arctic river rushing with the strength of family and place. As it widens to the family of Alaska's wild world, we witness one woman's courage to live the life that is her heart's deepest desire."

Marybeth Holleman, author of *tender gravity* and *The Heart of the Sound*

"A gorgeous evocation of what it means to be an Alaskan, rendered with great skill and artistry by a writer who loves this place and knows how to show it."

Rich Chiappone, author of *Hunger of Crows* and *Liar's Code*

Rivers and Ice

A Woman's Journey Toward Family and Forgiveness

Susan Pope

Riddle Brook Publishing
Peterborough NH

PCIP Data

Names: Pope, Susan, 1948- author.
Title: Rivers and ice : a woman's journey toward family and forgiveness / Susan Pope.
Description: Peterborough, NH : Riddle Brook Publishing, 2024.
Identifiers: LCCN 2023946902 (print) | ISBN 979-8-9859413-6-4 (trade paperback) | ISBN 979-8-9859413-7-1 (ebook)
Subjects: LCSH: Women--Biography. | Alaska--Biography. | Families. | Hiking. | Alaska--Description and travel. | Autobiography. | BISAC: BIOGRAPHY & AUTOBIOGRAPHY / Personal Memoirs. | BIOGRAPHY & AUTOBIOGRAPHY / Women. | FAMILY & RELATIONSHIPS / General.
Classification: LCC F910.7.P67 A3 2024 (print) | LCC F910.7.P67 (ebook) | DDC 979.8--dc23.

Portions of this book have appeared in various other publications. Please see the Acknowledgments at the end of the book for a complete list.

Library of Congress Control Number: 2023946902
ISBN: 979-8-9859413-6-4 (Paper); 979-8-9859413-7-1 (EPUB)

Cover photo by Jim Thiele
Cover design by Abdul Wahid
Copy Editing by Renee Charney

Riddle Brook Publishing, LLC
Peterborough, NH
www.riddlebrookpublishing.com

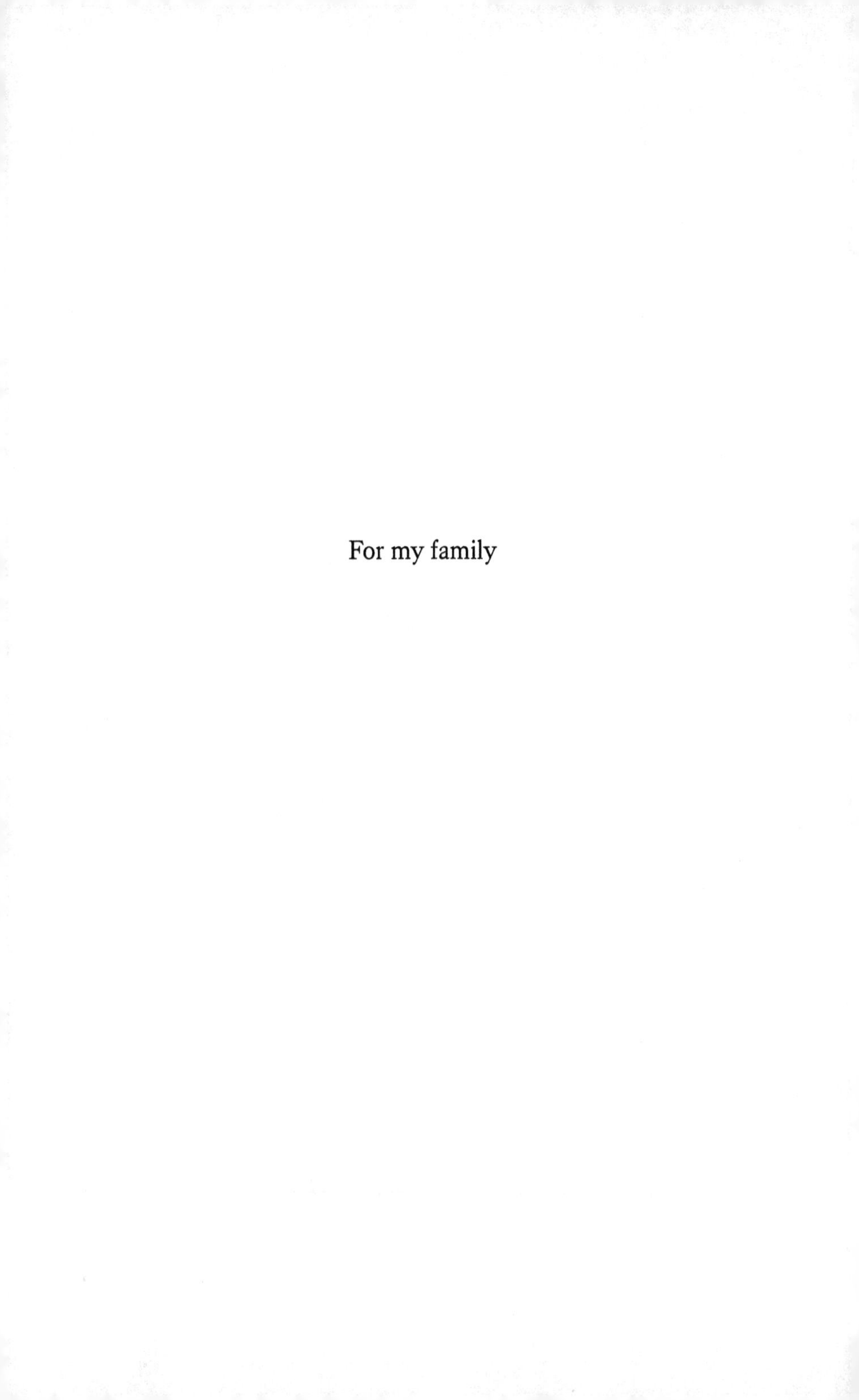

For my family

Prologue

Like the lame caribou we spied on the ridge yesterday, just a beat off the rhythm of the rest of the herd, I lagged behind my seven companions. Swaying back and forth, doing my best to stay upright, I slogged through a deep, water-filled trench sliced into the spongy North Slope tundra by generations of caribou hooves.

Five days into our ten-day raft trip on the Nigu River and we had seen no other humans. Only caribou, squirrels, grizzlies, foxes, peregrine falcons, songbirds, and bugs—all interspersed with the unpredictable Arctic squalls. But others had traveled before us. We'd discovered their signs atop ridges, along the hillsides, across the flats. Inupiat people hunted and fished seasonally across this terrain for thousands of years before whites arrived.

We were eight people, six paying customers—my husband Jim and I, longtime friend Pat, three men from outside of Alaska—and two guides, Jen and Bill.

I had my reasons for taking this trip, though I wasn't sure I could sort them all out. When I come to the Arctic I feel lost—small in a land so big. On this trip I hoped to become brave and strong, recover my true purpose, and reconnect with my husband. So far, I was not quite there.

Jim was on the horizon with the rest of the men. With his short legs, compact body, and the agility of a caribou, he easily kept up with the group's competitive pace. Jen waited for me beside a stream that tumbled down a notch in the rocks. I welcomed her company.

"Let's head up this draw," she suggested, pointing to the willow-lined "V" the creek had carved in the slope.

As the angle of the hillside steepened and a thin mist enveloped us, my heart thumped against my sticky shirt and throbbed inside my ears. Jen stopped with me while I caught my breath. We began our "how I came to Alaska" stories. I gradually shed layers of clothing while we traded memories of family, friends, loves, and travels—and discovered we were both writers.

During my childhood in urban Alaska, stories about the Arctic convinced me the terrain was too frigid, harsh, and barren for a person as weak as I imagined myself to be. Much later, my work drew me north, across the Brooks Range. As I flew above the changing hues and textures of the terrain, my eyes and heart began to open. It was early June and summer retreated beneath me. Bright yellow-green buds gave way to red-tipped twigs, then to last summer's smashed and faded grass, wind-drifted snow, and finally the great white ice ridges of the Arctic Ocean.

The land held so much more than the stark imaginings of my childhood. I wanted more.

The following summer Jim and I joined a river trip through the Arctic National Wildlife Refuge, and I began to explore the layers of life woven deep in the tundra.

After two years of saving, we returned. Before this trip began, a massive flood had ripped across this valley. Water tore new channels, ripped out chunks of tundra, and left a dark curtain of mud sagging from the willows. Shelves of black ice—melting permafrost—loomed above our heads on the riverbanks. Periodically, slabs of this muddy ice broke free and crashed into the river. Our ten-foot rafts, laden with gear, sometimes lodged in shallow channels and we were forced to get out to free them from the gravel. This happened more frequently in Jen's raft. Though she had traveled this river before, her partner Bill was more experienced at choosing the right course.

On a day when we traveled with Jen—Jim and I in the bow, Pat in the stern—our team repeatedly stalled on the river bottom. With Bill's muscle power the other team easily spun their raft around into safer water.

As we followed Bill's lead toward a deeper channel, we changed course abruptly and slammed against a hidden rock. I lurched forward, stopped from hurling into the river only by my toe jammed into the rubber strap in the bottom of the raft. My paddle flew into the current and bobbed down the river as the force of the water wedged us tight against the rocks beneath. With great bouncing and pushing, pulling and swearing, we finally broke free.

Absent my ability to paddle, our raft zigzagged erratically in the current. When we caught up to the other raft, eddied out against the shore, Bill waved my paddle. "Missing something?" Everyone laughed but me.

Exhaustion seeped in as adrenaline drained from my body. *This is too hard.* I thought. *I'm too soft. What am I doing here?* I grabbed my paddle back. Soon, my mood brightened as our team slipped into a perfect synchrony of motion.

***

By day eight of our trip, we had still seen no other people, but had seen hundreds of caribou—tiny calves fighting the current to cross the river with their mothers—grizzlies, and ground squirrels, the fundamental link in the Arctic food chain. But no wolves. Though we had seen their scat, they remained elusive.

I drifted more and more into Arctic time, my body embracing the light, the wind, the storms, and the river. By trial and error, I learned how to hike more efficiently on the tundra. Slide your feet around the tundra tussocks, not on top of them.

Facing into the wind, we crossed a gradually rising plain as tundra gave way to grassland. We reached the crest of a hill that bore a perfectly round crown of craggy boulders. We stood outside the circle, our murmurs drifting off with the wind until Bill stepped inside and crouched behind a rock. I followed his lead and slipped behind another boulder. Safe from the wind, I poked my head over the top of the rock. Scanning the full length of a massive lake below, I spotted scattered groups of caribou. It was the perfect place to hunt for game.

Down at the lake we discovered many shallow depressions in the grass around the shore—scars from ancient food caches dug into the permafrost, where food could be kept cold and even frozen beneath the permanently frozen earth. Beside one lay a chewed plank of wood, out of place in this treeless landscape. Bill lifted it up and we read the faded lettering across its weathered face: *Keep Out, Archaeological Site* and, even more faintly, the logo of a now-defunct oil company, left from oil exploration that occurred decades ago. This spot could have been a drilling pad.

We kept going, ascending the spine of yet another windswept ridge, this one worn smooth by generations of caribou seeking solace from their winged tormentors. Hugging the bare forehead of the bluff, backs turned to the wind, we found what we thought was a grave. Beside the caribou trail, a pile of gray-and-black lichen-covered river rocks had been carefully placed in the shape of a small adult or child. *Who was this person*, I wondered. *How did she or he die?*

I held back, peering deep into the spaces between the rocks, hoping to see a piece of hair or a swatch of caribou skin clothing. But the tidy pile of rocks revealed nothing, and we left them in peace. Beyond was the view that brought us to this ridge: a band of caribou bulls on the next bluff, the gray sinuous river, the silvery lakes, the luminous green of the tundra, and the volatile blue-and-white sky. Once, woolly mammoths grazed below. I scanned the terrain with my binoculars hoping to spot a wolf. No luck.

I opened my gritty eyes to the blue glow of our tent. Something was not right. Jim's rumpled sleeping bag lay empty. I heard small stones scraping against the sand outside, followed by a faint clicking. I sat up and fumbled for my boots. Yanking them on, I stepped outside in time to witness clouds scorched from below by the final gasps of the midnight sun—rose, tangerine, crimson. Jim, barefoot in his underwear, oblivious to the chill, shuffled in the sand of the former river channel where we camped. Head down, he peered into his old Nikon, perched on its scratched aluminum tripod. Without looking up, he said,

"It's almost there."

Jim, who once made his living as a photographer before he turned field biologist, then financial planner, never lost his unique eye for beauty in the natural world. I rubbed my eyes and shivered in my faded-blue long underwear.

As the clouds flared blood red, he waved a hand to chase away mosquitoes and squeezed off a few more shots. We watched the sunset pale to pink, then gray. Finally, Jim retrieved his camera from its perch and tucked it carefully into the case. I collapsed the old tripod and slid it beside the tent. As we crawled back into the warmth of our sleeping bags, I remembered why I fell in love with this man. Like a child, he dives into a moment of wonder—a sunset, a tiny catkin on a thumb-sized Arctic willow, the rainbow in a spider's dewy web—losing himself completely. And, sometimes, he pulls me with him.

Our last camp, near the confluence with the Colville River.

Hours of rain and wind pummeled us two nights ago. Because the tundra is just a thin spongy layer of vegetation sitting on top of frozen ground, a hard-driving rain quickly saturates that sponge, forming rivulets, then gushing streams, until finally dumping into rivers that spill out over the land.

At the start of the storm, we hauled our rafts upstream through a gentle-flowing, clear channel of the Etivluk River to a spot above a broad, rocky beach. Throughout the next day, even though the rain had stopped, this gentle side channel turned swift and brown. It flowed over land, joining the main channel, uniting into one frothing giant. As the river continued to rise, Jen and Bill took turns standing watch while the rest of us slept.

"Time to move!" Bill shouted sometime after midnight, We dashed to pick up tents, gear, and food, and remake camp at the base of the bluff. Any more water and we'd be climbing for our lives. But it stopped.

Two float planes were scheduled to pick us up yesterday at a gentle bend in the Colville River. But no planes were flying then or today. Jim and I scooped water from the river and took turns pumping the thick, cocoa-colored liquid through a filter, transforming it into a clearer, weak-tea version of water. We poured this silty tea over each other's heads. Although the frigid water burned my scalp and ears, I reveled in the simple pleasure of Jim's fingers on my neck and mine on his. With clean hair, I felt beautiful. I let my mind wander and tried again to figure out what brought me here and where I was going.

I thought of Dad. I was his first born, the son he never had, the only person in the family wild enough to make a trip like this. I never told him that my happiest childhood adventures were camping together beside a stream, him tossing a line into the water, a cigarette dangling from his half-smile, a couple of beer bottles stuffed in his pockets. He'd finish off a bottle, toss it into the woods, and start on another. I never figured out how he could love nature so much and yet treat it with such disrespect. To a city boy from Scranton, Pennsylvania, Alaska's wildness must have seemed endless. When I was in college, our arguments about the environment turned bitter. He never finished high school and I danced circles around him with my words. But he refused to back down.

"Men have to work," he'd say. "Jobs are more important than any damn trees or animals."

I'd fire back about ecosystems, the loss of one species is a loss for the planet, blah, blah, blah. I'd still be battling him.

"Hey!" Pat yelled, breaking the spell. "Look." He pointed to the water's edge, where a wet ring around a willow stick marked the high-water line. The river was slipping back from the bank. Bill called our bush pilot and learned that the weather was clear south of the Brooks Range, but we wouldn't get picked up that day. Too many other campers in the queue ahead of us.

The next day, I stumbled to the kitchen tent to fill my stained blue mug with coffee while Jim tore down our tent. Bill gestured toward the ridge behind us where a dark shape sat against the skyline. I peered through his spotting scope. A black wolf stared down at our camp. We had been watching for wolves the whole trip, but this was our first. I took this as a sign that my trip was complete. For several minutes we watched the wolf watch us. Finally, it rose, stretched, then disappeared behind the ridge. I grabbed my backpack, pulled out my journal, and scribbled out my return-home resolutions:

Take the grandkids camping
Fight to protect the Arctic
Publish the stacks of essays scattered on my desk
Get my body in better shape
Come back

I slid my journal into its plastic bag, stuffed it back into my daypack, waded into the water, and clipped my pack to the raft. I slid over the tube and took my place with Jim in the bow of the boat. Together, we heaved against the mud with our paddles as Jen and Pat shoved from the stern. We caught the current and floated free.

Part One

Chapter One

At the train station we paused for one final photo. Dad and Gramps in their dark fedoras, Mom and Ma (which was what we called our grandmother) in their Sunday wool coats, stockings, and best shoes. Mom, thin as a willow twig, leaned into her ample mother. Dad, a slight smile on his lips, held my one-year-old sister Patty in one arm, her white baby shoes resting against his overcoat. Gramps clamped his jaw tight and glared into the camera. He was losing his grandchildren. No more walks hand-in-hand with me to the neighborhood candy store, no more family dinners with all of us on Sunday after church. I was the only one in the picture with a full, teeth-revealing beam on my face.

We had been working for weeks to get ready to leave, selling our furniture, giving away my summer clothes and all but a few of my favorite toys. I was five years old and forced to say goodbye to my kindergarten class—there would be no kindergarten in Alaska—and my friends in our tightly crammed neighborhood. I did not fully grasp that my long walks and talks with Gramps were over, or that I would have no other kids to play with when I arrived in Alaska. Any grief at good-bye was displaced by the excitement of my first train ride, all the way across Canada, and the anticipation of my first air-plane flight. We were going to Alaska! Whatever that was.

My mother, born and raised in Buffalo, New York, whose travel ambitions rarely reached beyond Niagara Falls, was giving up all that was familiar to her because it was what her husband wanted. His chance at a better job, their chance at a better life, she told herself. Maybe she thought *What is wrong with what we have now?* but her husband wanted more. Back then, unions kept a tight fist on who got hired and who moved up. Maybe Dad refused to bribe someone, or maybe it was a post-war slump in the steel industry, but for some reason Dad could not keep steady work in Buffalo. A hard-working man, he wanted more for his family than a rented upstairs apartment in a house owned by someone else, behind another house owned by a different someone else. Even though he never finished high school, as a veteran he received funding to attend night classes to earn his electrician's certification. Alaska was a big risk, but a chance to land a solid job on his own merit, a chance to buy a house, and to live the life he dreamed of living after coming home from fighting a war.

But to his wife's family, the journey may as well have been to the other side of the world. Where the hell was Anchorage, Alaska, anyway? Wherever it was, they were sure they would never see their daughter or their grandchildren again. All they knew about Alaska came from movies like the *Call of the Wild* and *The Cheechahcos*.

My Irish grandma did not willingly relinquish ties to any of her five children. One boy was sent to Korea—she had no choice—but the rest still lived close by in Buffalo. Ma battled to keep her second daughter safe at home until my father found a job in Alaska and a place to live, and had saved enough money to bring the family North. Was she secretly hoping that maybe this man with his crazy ambitions would never send for his family and they would live with her forever?

But Gramps, in a rare stand against his domineering wife, said, "No!" His daughter's place, he argued, was with her husband, no matter how much they hated losing her. Case closed.

Off we went.

"Come to Alaska." Dad's father beckoned. "You'll find steady work here." Though the official population of Alaska was just around 130,000 then, and Anchorage a scant 11,000, the territory—not yet named the 49th state— was booming. With its proximity to Russia it was front and center in the Cold War. Skilled labor was needed to build, expand, and operate an extensive network of military bases, radar surveillance sites, and secret missile silos with weapons to shoot down any invading Russian air attacks and to target key sites within Russia.

My father's father had come to Alaska in 1947, working as a civil engineer on the military deep-water port of Whittier in Prince William Sound. Grandpa had lost his hand in an industrial accident when he was just seventeen, but this tragic disability opened doors to new opportunities. Through a rehabilitation program with the Depression-era Works Progress Administration, he studied to become a civil engineer. After his training, he worked remotely at sites all over the northeastern U.S. and Canada, returning home often for just a few weeks—enough time for his wife to get pregnant—then off again, each time leaving his wife to care for a family that eventually grew to ten children. When he was finally hired by the District Corps of Engineers on Ft. Richardson Army Base in Anchorage, he would at last settle in one place. But by that time, only his five youngest children remained at home.

After working for a year at his new Alaskan post, he sent for his wife and children. They traveled by bus from Delaware to Seattle, then caught a commercial flight on a re-purposed military plane from Seattle to Anchorage. There, the younger siblings settled into a life in the far north, a continent apart from their older brothers and sisters.

In the weeks before we left to join Dad's family in Alaska, Uncle Eddy, my mother's brother, had teased me incessantly, calling me "Eskimo Susie." "You'll have to live in igloos, eat seal meat, and wear fur boots and parkas all year because it's so cold," he said. I didn't quite believe him, but he was an adult, so something of what he told me must be true.

I was relieved when we landed in Anchorage and I spotted no igloos, only a small flat building with a big tower, the new international airport. And snow. He was right about that. When we left Buffalo, the grass and leaves were turning green, but here it was still winter.

My parents must have been exhausted. Five days on a train trying to keep two kids busy. Then days of layover in Edmonton, Alberta, waiting for a flight to Anchorage. I imagine they sometimes questioned the wisdom of their decision, giving up their modest working-class life, in a town, a neighborhood, they knew so well. In spite of reassurances from Dad's father and mother, was Alaska really where they should raise their kids, make a comfortable life for themselves?

When we finally arrived and climbed down the steep metal airplane steps into what passed for spring in 1954 pre-statehood Alaska, three strangers waited for us inside the crowded terminal. A heavy man with a cigar in his mouth reached out to hug my dad with one arm, the coat sleeve of his other arm dangling where his hand should have been. As Dad wrapped his arms around his father, I could hear the big man wheezing slightly. When he reached for me I drew back, afraid of his size and of what might be hidden beneath his sleeve. A woman with fuzzy brown hair pushed past him, kissed my cheek with her thin red lips, and squeezed me into her soft bosom. "I'm so glad you finally made it," she said. I relaxed in her embrace.

A tall boy hung back until the hugging and kissing were over, then shook hands with Dad. "This is my brother David," said Dad, "your uncle." Not present were Dad's sister Margie, who worked as a butcher in a grocery store downtown, Dad's brother Pat, who worked at the same store, and his other brother Bill, part of the ground crew working for one of the airlines at the airport.

For a few weeks we stayed with Dad's parents and three brothers in their government housing on Ft. Richardson. David was still in school, but Pat and Bill had dropped out of high school and lived at home while working. "I'm so happy to have girls around," Grammy told us. All her other grandchildren were back East, and she lived in a household of men. She pampered my sister and me, curling my hair, letting me put on her make-up, and allowing Patty to make a mess in the kitchen "helping" to make cookies.

Since Grandpa worked for the military, he qualified for base housing, but the rules were strict. No other extra residents were allowed besides those on the original rental agreement. Patty and I couldn't go outside and play, and we had to keep quiet. We couldn't stay there long, not with four extra people bumping against each other in an apartment with only one bathroom. We tried to stay out of view, but our presence was jeopardizing my grandparents' housing privileges.

Housing was in short supply in Cold War Anchorage. People lived in military surplus Quonset huts, basements with no top stories, houses always in progress with no interior walls, trailers, or crude log cabins. Wealthier residents lived downtown in tidy wooden houses with small yards.

After a couple of weeks my parents found an apartment in Spenard, a suburb of Anchorage, named for Joe Spenard, a bootlegging entrepreneur who in 1916 plowed his own road to a lake he named after himself and built an illegal resort on Forest Service Land. Spenard declared itself a separate town back then, with its own postal address, and a profusion of shady bars and strip joints operating away from the scrutiny of the downtown Anchorage business owners and city fathers. As Spenard grew up next to Anchorage, it retained much of its seedier origins but offered cheaper housing. Its neighborhoods had apartments and small houses on tiny lots (with an occasional after-hours gambling joint), a couple of elementary schools, a grocery store, a bowling alley, a business district with a few cafes and a string of bars where "B-girls," as they were called then, plied patrons—often soldiers from the military bases—for drinks and other favors.

Our cheap one-bedroom apartment was at the far western end of Northern Lights Boulevard about two miles from Joe

Spenard's original road, now a two-lane highway. We didn't know it when we moved in, but locals called our apartments the "rabbit hutches." Maybe it was their haphazard construction, or the raised wooden walkway connecting the buildings, or maybe the sharp contrast between our hovels and the expensive new development down the road called Turnagain-by-the-Sea. Since I had not yet learned to read the numbers on the doors, I sometimes burst into the wrong apartment, then halted in panic, sure that my family had deserted me in this strange and faraway land.

I quickly discovered that the rabbit hutches housed a different breed of kids than the ones in our Buffalo neighborhood. Here, while we played in the dirt and weeds between the walkways, kids said words I was told never to use and stole my toys. I watched with a mixture of admiration and disgust as they dug for treasures in the dumpsters out back. These were not the paved driveways or city sidewalks of Buffalo where I felt safe wandering just weeks ago.

With his father's knowledge of the civil service application process, Dad spent that summer filling out forms, describing every job he ever had and every class he had taken at night school, and in the spring of our second year in Alaska he finally landed a position at the power plant on the Air Force base. He bought our family's first car, the one he had been borrowing from his boss, and we rented a small house on a big lot—still in Spenard—closer to the airport, but farther away from grocery stores and businesses. We lived about a mile from a nightclub called the Idle Hour, which burned down every few years—arson was always suspected—and was rebuilt with new owners. A gas station about a half-mile away was the only other business nearby.

Our house had probably been built in the early 1940s, maybe the remnant of old homestead land, and had a long driveway stretching from what must have been a much quieter Spenard Road back when it was built. There were no close-by neighbors, just a few scattered houses closer to the lake. The place had been tenderly cared for by the older couple we rented from. They had planted poppies, bleeding hearts, lilacs, dahlias, and other flowers we couldn't name, and a large vegetable garden with rows of raspberry bushes supported by wooden stakes. An arctic entryway—which consisted of an outside door, a small alcove, and an interior door into the living room—enclosed its front entrance. Designed as a buffer between the icy outside air and the warmth of the interior, the entrance would freeze shut in the winter with snow piled against the outside door. But it added extra cold storage for anything that we didn't mind freezing. The place had one bedroom. Mom and Dad slept at one end, and my two-year-old sister Patty and I shared a bed at the other end. After the rabbit hutches, the house seemed like a mansion.

As the time to start school approached that fall, Mom discovered that my December birthday was too late to make the September cut-off to turn six and be eligible for first grade. I would have to wait another entire year before I could start. Since Mom didn't drive, we were stuck at home.

So much snow fell that first winter—134 inches—a record not broken until 2012. We were used to snow in Buffalo, of course. A blizzard would blast in and snow would pile up, shutting down schools and everything else. In a few days the town would clear the streets and sidewalks, sun would shine, and everything would melt. In Alaska, though, nothing stopped for the snow. The main roads got plowed, but work, school, and businesses mostly just carried on. People carried chains and shovels in their cars, and if they saw someone who was stuck or had slid into the ditch, helped them out.

I don't know what sustained my mother that first winter in Alaska, so far away from family and everything familiar, but even in the coldest weather she bundled us in snowsuits, scarves, mittens, and boots and hustled us outside. Our eyes teared in the wind and the sudden brilliance of the sun reflecting on all that white. We plopped into the fresh snow, waved our feet and hands to make angels or burrowed into the snowbanks along the walk pretending they were igloos. In much too short a time, Mom herded us back to the house. "It's too cold," she would say. "You'll frost your lungs." For years, I believed this was true.

As the winter wore on, a windstorm would descend, blowing a white-out, piling the snow into drifts which hardened like concrete. Moose ambled past our windows and gazed inside. To a city-bred five-year-old, this land was like the fairy tales my mother read to us, a magical place where anything was possible.

Someone had left skis in the garage of that rented one-bedroom house. Child-sized and made of wood, they had leather bindings that fit over any boots. I had never seen a pair of real skis before. Skiing was more magic, a sport for the movies and TV, rich people carving tracks through deep snow in faraway lands or racers weaving between gates at dizzying speeds down icy trails.

One weekend when fresh snow covered the hard-packed drifts, Dad asked if I wanted to go skiing.

"Yes!" I said, picturing myself swooping through the snow like the brightly dressed people I had seen on TV.

Dad pulled the skis from the shelf in the garage and dusted them off. There were no poles to go with them. We trudged through the snow to the top of the hill behind the house. Trusting him completely, I let him strap the skis on my snow boots and nudge me down the slope. The slick-bottomed skis slid out from under me. Plop. Snow in my face, down my neck, up my sleeves. Dad hoisted me out of the snow, stood me up again, then pointed me down the hill.

Plop. Again and again, he hauled me out of the snow, propped me up, started me down the hill, always with the same result. Snow packed inside my boots, hat, and mittens.

Skiing was much harder than I imagined. "Daddy, please. I want to go in," I begged. "I don't want to ski."

Neither of us had any idea that skis required wax, that poles made it easier to balance, that maybe we should have started on a flat surface. Dad shook his head. I knew he was disappointed that I gave up. He wanted me to keep trying until I reached the bottom on my own. Finally, he unhooked the skis and put them back into the garage for the next kid whose family rented the house. Neither of us ever asked to bring out the skis again.

Though Dad had never skied, on the ice he transformed into someone I had never seen before. I discovered this after Christmas, when my parents gave me a pair of bright white figure skates and Dad promised to teach me how to skate. Surely there were ice rinks in Buffalo, but I don't remember our family ever skating while we lived there. Was there not enough time, or money, or was a rink too far away to reach on foot or by bus? I don't know.

One weekend Dad and I drove the mile or so to the lake, where locals reserved a small section of shoreline (in an area not used by ski planes in winter), for skating and swimming. Dad held my hand as I teetered on my skates. With winter daylight so brief, we skated mostly in the dark, relying on the snow to reflect enough light from the surrounding neighborhood to find our way around the lake. The air stung my cheeks and frost coated my eyelashes. I fell often, but with padded snow pants, I scrambled up again without much damage. Kids and adults whizzed around us, and periodically Dad would break away and skate on his own, swift, fluid, and elegant in his black hockey skates, carving the ice with heavy blades, kicking up a wake of powdered snow. Skates transformed him into a handsome, glamorous stranger. Graceful. Elegant. Carefree. Growing up, his family lived for a few years in a resort town on Lake Erie. When the summer residents packed up and left for the season, the few remaining kids had the place to themselves. When the lake froze over, there was not much to do but skate. Dad and his friends amused themselves by leaping over barrels on the ice. No hockey, no organized sports, no money for pucks or sticks.

As my skating skills improved, Dad would grab my hand and we would coast together, dancing side-by-side. I pretended we were one of the couples in the *Ice Capades*, a traveling ice skating show broadcast on television. Wanting to skate as well as he did, I imitated his smooth glide, side-to-side. At first, I was clumsy, teetering on the sharp, slippery blades. Gradually, I got better. After many times, I became steady enough to skate in step with him. I was only six, but here was a grownup thing I could do. We were partners. I was his girl—graceful, beautiful, loved.

Mom adjusted to life on the Last Frontier without her extended family. I'm sure Grammy, my dad's mom, offered advice, and I remember occasionally Dad would drop Patty and me off at their house so my parents could do something without us. But, since we lived at opposite ends of town and neither woman could drive, we rarely saw my Alaskan grandparents.

Mom grew up in a family of five kids in a neighborhood of buses, corner groceries and taverns, and the parish church down the street. She had no need to learn to drive. She often talked about how when she was growing up her mother never let her do anything. She was not allowed to cook or do any of the domestic chores women at the time were supposed to do. Certainly, during the economic hardship of the Great Depression, Mom's help was needed, but her mother was impatient and critical, so Mom was reluctant to try new things.

From a family of ten kids, and with his father gone most of the time, Dad had no choice but to learn independence early on. He quit school to help support his family before joining the military. Dad always teased Mom that he had to teach her how to cook and take care of a household when they got married. She never disagreed with him about this. At our new home in Alaska, she had a lot to learn.

That first summer in our Lake Spenard house, Mom and Dad took advantage of the already-plotted vegetable garden at the house with the sloping yard and planted lettuce, peas, carrots, onions, cabbage, potatoes, and beets. Raspberries ripened on stalks nearly as tall as me. Mom had developed a friendship with Grace, the wife of Dad's boss. As a young woman, Grace had moved to Alaska from her home in Quebec, speaking only French, learning English along the way, working waitress jobs, on one of which she met her husband. Together they had three children.

People came to Alaska then for a variety of reasons. Some were escaping—bills, the law, spouses, families. Others were running toward something—a better life, like us, or a chance to start over where no one knew them, or a chance to make fast money. Often single women, discovering the outsized ratio of men to women in Alaska, came to find husbands. Grace knew a lot about survival in this foreign land and willingly shared her expertise with my mom.

One fall morning while Dad was at work, my two-year-old sister Patty and I headed off with Mom into the woods behind our house to pick berries. Mom carried an empty coffee can, while Patty and I carried smaller plastic containers. With jackets, jeans, and rubber boots, we were dressed for the damp, cold September weather. Frost had already wiped out the last of the garden peas. Mom had tied her wispy hair back with a red and blue scarf. The tart, heady scent of high-bush cranberries pierced the morning air, forever imprinting on my brain the tangy wet-earth smell of late Alaska fall.

We crossed the lawn, last night's frost slowly melting away, and waded into tall grass that soaked our pants and jackets. We tromped through the thick underbrush into the woods, Mom lifting Patty over fallen trees, scooting her past the prickly devil's club growing at shoulder height. I trailed along, not sure what we were looking for, but watching out for the bull moose with the giant antlers we spotted yesterday, devouring the last of Mom's cabbages.

"Look at all these berries," Mom said. The plump, translucent, ruby berries hung in clusters against serrated leaves bigger than my six-year-old hands. "I think these are high bush cranberries," Mom said.

We began picking. Patty popped one in her mouth.

"Yuck." She puckered her lips and spat it out. I tried one. The taste reminded me of throwing up.

"I'm not eating any jam with these berries," I said.

"Grace said they need lots of sugar," Mom replied.

Patty and I picked and dumped, picked and dumped, from our smaller bins into Mom's coffee can. As we turned back toward the house, Mom entrusted me with the full can of berries while she lifted Patty over and around the deadfalls and scraggly black spruce. I held the can with both hands close to my chest, afraid I would tumble and lose all we had worked to gather. We eased carefully back down the slick grass on the hillside and when we reached our lawn, we were thoroughly soaked from top to bottom.

"Give me the berries," Mom ordered as Patty skittered to the sidewalk beside the house. I handed them to her, relieved that I was no longer in charge of making sure they didn't spill. Mom and I squeezed past the empty chicken coop, stepping on an old piece of plywood to avoid a puddle. Suddenly Mom slid across the slimy wood, falling backwards and clunking her head with a loud thunk against the board. The berry bucket flew out of her hand, sending the perfect little balls exploding into the air and rolling into the grass, into the puddle, and under the chicken wire.

Mom lay with her eyes closed.

"Mommy!" I shouted. "Are you okay?"

No answer. Patty scurried back from the sidewalk on her fat little legs. We leaned over Mom, her soft brown curls unleashed from the knotted scarf that lay on the plank beside her.

"Mommy sleep?" Patty whispered.

I couldn't hear Mom breathing.

"Get up, Mommy!" I yelled, this time louder.

What should I do? Patty and I were alone. Dad was far away at work. Our nearest neighbors were down the long sandy road that led to the lake. It was my fault, I knew, because I didn't catch Mom.

At that moment, I must have realized that Mom was not immortal. Something could happen to her, and I would have to take care of myself and Patty. Dad would have to work, and we'd be left on our own. My life was in my own hands.

Mom's eyes flickered. She moaned.

"Wake up, Mommy." I held out my hands. She opened her eyes and stared straight up at the cloudy sky. Slowly she sat up, shook her head, and rubbed the back of her neck.

"Oh, look at our berries," she said.

Red orbs bobbed in the brown puddle like cherries on top of a root beer float. I planted my feet, grasped her hand, and helped steady her as she got up. She staggered, tried to brush the mud from her jeans, and stooped to retrieve the few stray berries visible in the thick grass. At that moment, I knew how fragile she was, and how tenuous our life was in this big new place.

Chapter Two

During that long winter, it turned out to be a good thing the district's age requirements kept me from attending school.

When Dad left for work, he turned off the stove, but the coffee pot was still hot. I knew just how Mom liked her coffee and it was my job to bring it to her every morning as she sat up and smoked her first cigarette. Her special cup, white on the outside, muddy-looking on the inside, sat on the counter top. I poured the liquid from the big metal pot, careful not to fill it to the top. I liked the burnt, bitter smell. Next, I took a spoon from the silverware drawer, dipped it into the sugar bowl, and sprinkled the white crystals into the dark brown drink. I watched them sparkle, then disappear. I turned to the refrigerator, pulled it hard until I heard the latch pop, then found the can with the cow on it. I poured the creamy yellow milk from the tiny hole until the coffee turned the color of caramel candy and I stirred it. With both hands, I carried the cup into the bedroom and handed it to Mom.

Coffee delivered, my next job was to keep Patty from jumping on Mom's bed or escaping out the door or marking the walls with her crayons. Mom was not allowed to get out of bed except to go to the bathroom. Sometimes she leaned on me, and I helped her into the bathroom. If Patty took a nap, Mom sometimes read to me. I didn't know what was wrong with her. I knew it wasn't measles or mumps because she had no lumps or bumps on her skin. Maybe it was polio, so much in the news and on television back then. I thought she might have to go into an iron lung.

When Dad came home from work each day, I helped him fix dinner, clean up, and do the laundry. I didn't know when Mom would get up again. I missed playing with her, going outside, coloring, helping her make bread. But also, I was proud to be Dad's helper, a big girl. I could take care of Mom.

I don't remember how long Mom stayed in bed that year. What I found out later, as an adult, was she had been pregnant. Something went wrong long before her due date; the baby's heartbeat grew faint, then gone—I never got the full story—and the Catholic hospital sent her home to bed, in case, against all odds, the fetus was still viable. There she stayed until spontaneously aborting the baby. I never knew the grief my parents must have felt, or the effort it took to shield my sister and me from what had happened.

The next fall I was thrilled to finally start school. I would learn to read and have a chance to play with other kids. But getting there became a problem. Though a school bus passed right by our driveway, we were not far enough from the school to qualify for a ride.

Walking to school was dangerous for a first grader along a busy road with no shoulder. Also, packs of loose and feral dogs roamed the area, some likely carrying rabies. Dad left for work long before school started. Mom didn't drive, so at first she walked me to school every day, holding my hand, carrying Patty on her hip. As the days grew shorter and darker, and Patty grew heavier, Mom began leaving her at home while she walked me to school. When she discovered Patty was making phone calls while she was gone and talking on the party line, Mom asked the gas station owner down the road to take me to school when he drove his own kids. Then she only had to walk the half-mile to the station, where the family also lived. But I got in trouble with my teacher because we always arrived late. Finally, a taxicab company offered to round up all the stray kids who didn't qualify for the school bus and take us to school each day for a fee. I could arrive at school without fear of being punished for being late.

I awakened one night to the sound of my mother weeping. I had never heard my mother or any other adult cry. I lay still, straining to understand the words distorted by her sobs. She was on our only phone in the living room.

"Dead . . ." I heard her say.

Who had died? I wanted to jump out of bed and find out, but I was too scared. Finally, Mom tiptoed through the bedroom on her way to the bathroom.

"Mommy, what's wrong?" I called out.

"Oh, Susie," she said. "Grammy and Grandpa died in a car crash. Your Uncle David is still alive but very hurt."

My grandparents had been traveling the Alcan Highway back to Alaska from visiting family on the east coast. Back then, the Alaska-Canada highway was gravel and notoriously dusty. The two cars collided head-on near Whitehorse, Yukon Territory—no one ever figured out who was at fault—and my Uncle David was the only survivor. I have no memory of a funeral or the grief my parents must have felt at the loss of their Alaskan family. I only remember the upheaval ripping the fabric of our family apart.

Weeks later, I came home from school to find my youngest uncle, fifteen-year-old David, in the living room, staring out the window, a bandage across his forehead, a red gash across the bridge of his nose, and dozens of cuts along his jaw line. He tried to say hello, but he couldn't open his mouth because his jaw was wired shut, so only a grunt emerged. I dashed from the room and hid behind my bed, wanting nothing to do with the spooky creature who'd come back from death.

Soon he was joined by his brothers (who could no longer live in the duplex their parents had been renting on Government Hill, near the military base). Now our one-bedroom house had to accommodate two more people in addition to David, leading to blankets and sleeping bags, shirts and blue jeans, shoes and underwear, the evidence of smelly teenage boys strewn all over our house. I became the little sister they'd never had. Sometimes they played with me—building with Lincoln Logs, tossing balls, or shooting marbles. But just as often I was the victim of their relentless teasing when they played catch with my dolls, made fun of the way I talked, or hid my toys in places I couldn't reach. I must have been a distraction from their grief, but I felt like there was nowhere for me to escape, Mom and Dad so preoccupied with trying to navigate their new responsibilities. I didn't know where I fit into this new chaotic family; no longer the oldest responsible child, I became just another little kid.

A few months later, we were forced to leave the house with the beautiful yard. The woods, the house, the garden would all be razed to build a new hotel.

Grimy snow still clung to the brown grass when we pulled up at our new house in the heart of residential Spenard. The morning breeze carried the damp, heady scent of Alaskan spring—hope and melting dog dung. Heated by a smelly oil stove that took up most of the living room, the house was a two-bedroom box, painted steel gray inside and out. But it was ours, the first home my parents had ever owned. I'm not sure how they scraped together the money for the house. Maybe it was the freelance electrical jobs my dad took on some weekends.

My sister and I would share a bed in the walk-in closet off my parents' bedroom, and my Uncle David would take over the second bedroom located off the living room. (After his long recovery, David moved to Seattle briefly to live with his older brother Gene, who had not migrated to Alaska with his younger siblings. David missed Alaska, so returned to live with us, finishing high school and later joining the navy.) Dad, as the oldest sibling in Alaska, somehow felt it was his responsibility to take care of David after their parents' death. Dad's other Alaskan brothers, Pat and Bill, were living on their own by then, but often used our house as a home base and showed up for meals, to do laundry, or to work on their cars.

Our new house had a fenced yard, and there was a grocery

store down the street, a bowling alley a block away, and other kids nearby. Best of all, I could walk around the neighborhood and to school all by myself.

While the grownups moved furniture into our new house, Mom scribbled a grocery list on a piece of paper and sent me to the store. I had never been to any store by myself. She trusted me. I pulled on my rubber boots and turquoise parka, then headed toward the big concrete store at the end of the block. Puddles dotted the muddy street. Giddy with freedom, I splashed from one to another. Water ran down ditches on both sides of the dirt road, little streams with floating pop cans, Popsicle sticks, paper cups. I edged to one side to watch the flow, easing my boots closer and closer to the lip of the trench. Then with one spectacular tumble, I lost my footing and plunged into the water.

Stunned, I sat gasping for a few seconds, up to my neck in frigid water. Then I scanned the street for witnesses. My first day in my new neighborhood, my first solo trip to the store, and I'd made a fool of myself. Surely our new neighbors were staring at me through their windows and laughing, but I saw no kids outside, no cars on the street, no adults in their yards. Saved from humiliation, I kneeled on the ice-slickened bottom of the ditch, crawled to one side, then clawed my way to solid ground, standing on shaking legs. Water poured from my parka and sloshed in my boots as I stumbled back toward the house, trying not to cry.

My mom ordered me to change clothes, handed me a fresh grocery list, and sent me off again. This time I succeeded. I walked through the door into a grown-up world that was frightening, but also a relief from the turmoil in which our family had been living. I found the milk and bread and cheese that were on my list, handed the clerk my mother's note giving me permission to buy her a pack of cigarettes, (which he put in a separate bag), relinquished my money, and walked back home with my prizes. Over the next months and years, I would retrace the steps to the store and back hundreds of times. I would fall in love with the boxboys who carried the ladies' groceries out to their cars, and I would grow old enough to be denied that pack of cigarettes, even with a note.

With their bare hands, Mom and Dad worked to transform the shabby little house and scruffy yard into a respectable middle-class home. They planted a garden, painted the place in bright colors, and built a third bedroom by tearing down the walk-in closet where Patty and I slept and constructing a wall to create a real bedroom with a door. They replaced the drippy oil stove in the living room with a forced-air furnace. This required them to dig a crawl space under the house, which they did by hand, Dad using pick and shovel, Mom hauling buckets of dirt out of the hole. Though Mom was a traditional 1950s' homemaker, she was not afraid to get her hands dirty or pitch in to do manual labor.

In addition to home remodeling skills, Mom and Dad learned to benefit from the bounty provided by the vast landscape surrounding us. With his co-workers at the plant as mentors, Dad took up hunting—sheep, moose, caribou, and even spruce grouse. With the help of my Aunt Margie, trained as a butcher, Mom learned to carve wild game into steaks, roasts, and stew meat, and to pluck feathers from grouse. I'm sure she never envisioned this for her life, but she also never shared any misgivings with me or talked about missing her family.

Our neighborhood, within a grid of gravel streets named after presidents—Cleveland, Roosevelt, Taft, Harding,

McKinley and others—was bounded by two busy highways and a railroad track. Occasionally, my best friend Judy and I would sneak out of its bounds to roam the tracks, following them into the wilds beyond the Tudor Road industrial zone, where we could still glimpse the wilderness that must have been there when Joe Spenard cut his road from downtown Anchorage. Listening to my dad tell stories of his adventures as a boy in upstate New York camping in the woods with his brothers, Judy and I dreamed of hauling our sleeping bags to the woods beyond the neighborhood and camping on our own.

"No," Dad said. "Girls don't do that."

"Why?" I asked. It wasn't fair.

He never gave me a good reason, but I guessed he thought the world was just too dangerous for a girl to roam on her own.

This protectiveness spilled over into another means I hoped would help me escape the house and join my friends—bike riding.

"No girl of mine is going to ride a bike," Dad declared. "She might get herself killed."

I didn't understand why riding a bike was such a threat. Had he witnessed a bike accident in which a child was hurt or killed? Did he think girls could not ride bikes as well as boys? Or did he doubt that drivers in our town would watch out for children on bikes? Once again, he didn't explain his reasons.

The years wore on, and though my begging left him unswayed, I did what I wanted anyway. At twelve, I borrowed a bike from Judy's younger brother and slipped into the alley behind our street to teach myself how to ride a bike. "Look at the big girl on the teeny bike!" some kids yelled. I didn't care. The humiliation was worth it when feet, peddles, balance, and determination all worked in tandem, and I coasted to freedom down the dusty, rutted alley. From then on, I shamelessly borrowed bikes from other kids in the neighborhood and peddled the streets with my friends. My mother must have known about my surreptitious rides since our kitchen window looked out into the alley, but she said nothing.

Dad had strict rules about what girls weren't supposed to do, but he did take us camping. On a Friday evening we would have everything ready by the time he came home from work—Army surplus tent and sleeping bags, mosquito repellent, camp stove, hot dogs, hamburgers, and, as a treat, soda pop and the makings for s'mores—all to spend a weekend on the Kenai Peninsula, a three-hour drive away. A pillow, pajamas, doll, and book, and I was ready to leave. Patty and I crawled onto a mattress covering the back of the station wagon amongst all the food and gear. As we drove down the Sterling Highway to Kenai Lake, or Crescent Creek, or the beach at Anchor River, I stared out the windows at the peaks never completely free of snow and dreamed of climbing them or hiking along the many trails marked by signs along the highway.

I spent most of my summertime bored, roaming the neighborhood with Judy, or lying in my bunk in my room reading book after book from the library. But a weekend in the woods meant exploration and freedom. We would set up camp, then gather wood for a fire. I belonged to a Brownie, then Girl Scout troop, and had learned how to build a fire with only twigs, birch bark, and a match. I wanted Dad to recognize my outdoors skills, so I would volunteer to start the fire, but I usually failed. With damp wood, damp bark, and damp matches, I'd barely generate a flicker. Mom would optimistically add newspaper, but this also failed. Dad, running out of patience, would douse the wood with charcoal lighter, and poof! ignition.

It was here I felt totally free: beside a river or a lake while Dad fished and Mom sat by the fire reading a book, while Patty and I roamed the campground and surrounding trails.

Chapter Three

I was eight, sitting in front of the TV with Dad's sister Margie and her husband, Uncle Dominic. After my grandparents died, this childless couple sometimes gave my parents a break and cared for Patty and me in their tiny spotless apartment near the military base. Though they did not have any real toys, they kept us busy with puzzles, colored pencils and paper, and experimenting with Margie's ample supply of cosmetics.

That night, they came to our house. Hours ago, Dad had taken Mom to the hospital because she was going to have a baby. Patty was already in bed, but because I was the oldest, they let me stay up. We had been getting ready for the baby for months.

We had a crib, clothes, diapers, and cuddly little toys. I hoped it was a girl because I didn't really like boys. Just when I was falling asleep, with my head on Aunt Margie's lap, I heard Dad's car pull up in the driveway. I rushed to the door and opened it.

"Is it a boy or girl?" I asked.

He didn't look at me but took off his coat and hung it on a hook by the door.

"Susie." He shook his head. "The cord was wrapped around the baby's neck."

"What do you mean?"

"They couldn't get him breathing."

Him. Dad wanted a son.

"Oh Paul," said Aunt Margie. "I'm so sorry."

"How is Dorothy?" Dominic asked.

"She's okay. Sleeping now."

Dominic and Margie stood for a long time looking at Dad. Behind us I heard the sounds of gunshots and galloping horses on the TV. I stared at my dirty socks.

"Well, I guess we should go home," said Dominic finally. "Let us know if we can help with the kids again."

They gathered their things and left Dad and me alone in the middle of the living room. I wanted to ask him more about what happened with the baby. He switched off the TV and headed into the kitchen. I followed him and watched as he reached into the cupboard for his bottle of whiskey, poured some into his tiny glass, and gulped it down in one swallow. Then, another one.

I didn't understand what had happened to the baby. I waited for him to tell me more, but he just sat at the table with his glass. Finally, I got up to leave.

"Good night, Dad.

"Night, Susie."

I slid into bed beside Patty and heard the hiss of her breath through baby teeth. She smelled like the chocolate ice cream we had for dessert. I pulled the covers up to my chin and tried to sleep but couldn't. I kept wondering what the hospital did with a dead baby. I wondered if Mom would bring him home to bury, or would the hospital take care of that. Patty pulled the covers off me in her sleep. I pulled them back and grabbed hold of her stuffed puppy.

It must have been almost morning when Dad peeked his head into the bedroom. When he leaned down to tuck me in, he smelled like cigarettes, whiskey, and sweat.

"What happened to the baby, Dad?" I asked.

"He couldn't breathe, Susie," he said.

I pictured a baby choking as they pulled him out of Mom's stomach. The doctor should have done something. Maybe the baby was already dead when he came out. I wonder what he looked like. Did he feel anything?

I was thinking these things when I leaned my head on Dad's shoulder and started to cry. I blubbered and slobbered until his shirt was soaking wet. He said nothing, only held me. I didn't know if he cried, because I heard nothing but the sound of my own sniffling and choking. Patty slept through it all.

"Would you tell your sister what happened?" he said finally.

"Sure."

I was old enough to deliver this sad news to my four-year-old sister. He trusted me. I woke her up and explained what I didn't fully understand—the cord, the strangling, death. She mumbled and just rolled over. In the morning she didn't remember I had given her the news and I'm sure Dad thought I never told her. I had let him down.

Dad put the baby clothes away somewhere while Mom was gone. He took the empty crib apart and hid it too. When she came home, we didn't talk about the baby or how sad we were. I didn't want to upset her. Neither did anyone else.

Dad never held me like that again.

After the death of my baby brother, our extended Alaskan family grew. Dad's brothers Bill and Pat married and eventually had six children each. Margie and Dominic later had two children. Dad must have seen himself as the patriarch, responsible for keeping the family together. We usually gathered at Christmas for a potluck at someone's house, and on Mother's Day when Dad would designate a campground or park close to town for a family picnic. I dreaded the Christmas gatherings when I was called upon to help with the toddlers and preschoolers, but loved the picnics even though they were usually cold and muddy so early in the season. Mom complained to me before each gathering. She had to do all the work to prepare and clean up. There was another reason, I realized later—she also dreaded the gatherings. Eventually, as any get-together wore on, Dad would have too much to drink and get into an argument with his brother Pat about unions. Pat was a dispatcher with the Teamsters union, a powerful position, especially when the Trans-Alaska Oil Pipeline was being built. Dad had never set aside his hatred of unions. Even as an eight- or ten-year-old, I was embarrassed by Dad's slurred words and his outsized anger as he and his brother repeated the same quarrel every time.

Alcohol was always present. Before I even started elementary school, Dad would pour me a shot glass full of beer or mix me a tiny glass of whiskey and 7Up while he drank his cocktail. During elementary school I was allowed small glasses of wine on special occasions. I never gave much thought about drinking alcohol. Dad had a beer every night after work, and sometimes three or four or five.

Eventually this grew into a problem. Dad was paid every other week and the paychecks were handed out at the plant on payday. He and a few coworkers began to stop at a local Spenard bar called the Buckaroo Club to cash their checks and have a few drinks. Sometimes Dad would come home long past dinner time, bringing toys for Patty and me and a flower for Mom. I was excited to receive the toys, but sensed the unspoken tension between my parents so I didn't quite feel right about the gift. Though I never heard Mom and Dad fight about this or even discuss it, at some point Mom arranged for Dad's checks to be mailed to our house. The first time one arrived in the mail, she pulled out an insurance form Dad had signed from a folder and gave me a blank piece of paper to practice his signature until I could reasonably duplicate it. After that I forged all of Dad's paychecks so she could take them to the bank and deposit them. I felt a bit guilty, knowing that signing for Dad was not quite right, but figured it was necessary to buy enough groceries to last until next payday.

We were Catholics. My sister and I attended catechism classes every Saturday, studied to receive First Communion, and later were confirmed in the church. Except for attending Mass every Sunday, though, and the ceremonies associated with communion and confirmation, we didn't participate in any other church activities—no novenas, Good Friday Stations of the Cross, even church picnics. In fact, we were what I'd call *pragmatic* Catholics. If someone invited us to dinner on a Friday night and they served meat (it was a mortal sin to eat meat on Fridays then), my parents told us not to be rude and to eat it anyway, and if we were camping or traveling it was okay to skip Mass on Sunday. So I was surprised when Dad volunteered to help raise funds to start the first Catholic school in Anchorage. A fund-raising committee organized a door-to-door campaign to seek out pledges from parishioners. For some reason, the committee decided, rather than start the school with kindergarten or first grade, it would start with middle school. Maybe the reasoning was because the teenage years were crucial in molding young Catholic minds into lifetime church members. With what must have been a colossal effort (considering the small population of Catholics in Anchorage), and perhaps with additional funding from outside of Alaska, the committee raised enough money to build the school, to be run by the Sisters of Providence, supplemented with lay teachers.

I was just beginning seventh grade when the school opened, so I entered its first class. All students were tested upon entering; I was placed in the college track. Before, although I loved school, I had never thought much about college. No one in our family had been to college, and the only women I knew who had attended college were my elementary school teachers.

The nuns were an anomaly to me. I had rarely encountered them aside from occasionally at Mass on Sunday or at the Catholic-run hospital. At my new school they became unlikely role models. With their flowing black robes, starched white wimples, and softly clicking rosary beads, they moved with grace and appeared serene. (Except for the chalk-throwing mustached Sister Michaeleen, the algebra teacher). They were smart, educated, articulate women, though in an entirely separate category from other women. Sister Mary Margaret, the young beautiful English teacher popular with her female students, was the first person to suggest I was college material. "Susan, you are smart. You should go to college," she said. A seed was planted, but when I shared this with my father, he said, "Forget it. I'm not spending my money for a girl to go to college. They just get married and waste it." Then why, I wondered, did he praise my good grades and spend the money to send me to Catholic school? Dad didn't even finish high school, let alone attend private school. Over and over, he told the story of how hard it was for him to learn his trade, working at the steel plant during the day and then attending electrical school at night. He complained about the college boys—those engineers, he called them—who bossed him around at the power plant, "but don't know shit," he said. Real work was done with your hands.

But Dad read. That's one thing we had in common. Books in our laps, beside our beds, stacked in the living room: mine from the library—Laura Ingalls Wilder, Louisa May Alcott, and later, teen romances—his from the grocery store, cheap paperbacks—Louis L'Amour, Mickey Spillane and other Westerns and murder mysteries. We both escaped into distant worlds of adventure and intrigue.

The summer before entering the ninth grade I lay on the living room sofa, my long bony feet sticking over the edge with a book in my face. I hated my thin, oily hair. Even though I slept in curlers all night, my hair went limp as soon as I took them out. My chest was flat and two top teeth thrust out from my gums like fangs. Pimples covered my face. My best friend Judy had long, thick black hair, clear pink skin, and big breasts. When we walked to the store, boys stopped to chat with her but ignored me.

One afternoon, Mom and our neighbor, Helen, sat at the white Formica kitchen table—so popular in the 1960s—drinking coffee and smoking. Though Mom often complained about Helen's too-frequent visits, gossiping, and intrusive questioning, she was the only person in the neighborhood with whom Mom regularly spent time.

"This one is healthy." I heard Mom tell Helen. "I'm taking shots so the pregnancy won't turn out like the others."

"God bless you, Dorothy," said Helen. "I would have gone crazy with all those lost babies."

"Paul wants a boy," Mom said. "I just want a healthy baby."

I was certain all my friends knew my mom was pregnant, mostly because Mom had never learned to drive and we had to walk everywhere—to church, the store, the bus stop, downtown. Mom was a thin person, so with the baby due in September, her stomach stuck way out. Dad was in Texas for a month, learning how to use some new machinery for the plant. My friends' mothers were finished having babies. Mom was the embarrassing proof my parents still had sex.

When I get my driver's license, I thought, *I'm not hanging around here. I'm not going to be a housewife like Mom, trapped at home, waiting for other people to take me places.*

When not preoccupied with my own grievances, I hoped the new baby would be healthy, that Mom would not have to endure the loss of another child. Mom and Dad never talked about the dead babies. Sometimes, though I wasn't very religious, I thought of them as angels, or maybe ghosts, drifting over our family.

Every four years, as part of my father's contract with the Air Force power plant, the government paid for us to visit family back East. (Alaska was considered an overseas post). We would spend three or four weeks in a dizzying flurry of visits to relatives in Buffalo, Scranton, and Baltimore. In Buffalo, we always stayed with Ma and Gramps, my mother's parents. On our last visit east, Ma requested we visit the cemetery where most of Mom's relatives were buried. As we walked across the neatly trimmed grass among the headstones in the hot sun, Ma told stories of each relative whose grave we passed. Just as my sister Patty began to cry she was sick and could not walk another step, we paused at a simple cross with letters that read simply "Baby Boy Janis." (Janis was our family name.)

"That's your baby brother," said Ma.

"What?" I wasn't sure if I heard her right.

Patty sat down in the shade of a nearby headstone. Mom gazed at the cross for a few minutes and stepped away.

"Your mother had other babies that didn't live," Ma said.

Mom had given birth to other babies while we still lived in New York. I had no memory of it. Stunned, I couldn't believe it.

"What happened to them?" I asked Ma.

"Only God knows," she said.

I pictured a bigger family than just us four, a brother closer to my age than the four years between Patty and me. What would it have been like to have a brother? I wanted to ask more, but Ma leaned down to me and said, "Let's not upset your mother," and we moved on. I learned I should not talk about these things with my mother.

Just as I entered the ninth grade, my sister Teri was born, a healthy eight pounds, and fifteen years younger than me.

Chapter Four

The next spring, on Good Friday, March 27, 1964, we were just sitting down at the kitchen table for a special dinner of king crab, a rare and expensive treat. We heard a rumble, then the rattling of dishes.

We sat still waiting for it to finish. Earthquakes were relatively common—Anchorage generally gets two or three minor ones every month—and are usually over in seconds. But this time, instead of the initial jolt and a rapid decrease, the shaking accelerated. Plants on the windowsill above the table tumbled down, spilling dirt into our special dinner. Cupboard doors opened and the dishes crashed to the floor. As the amplitude increased, so did the noise. Pictures crashing to the floor, lamps falling over, furniture knocking into the walls, the floor beneath us rolling. It did not stop. Dad grabbed Teri from her highchair and yelled, "Out of the house!" Struggling to stay upright, no time for shoes, we ran out onto the front sidewalk which was covered in snow. Around us, other neighbors popped out of their houses and stood in their driveways or on their front steps. Our station wagon, parked beside the house, leaped and jiggled as the ground bucked and shimmied. I believed we were going to die and began reciting the Act of Contrition, what every Catholic child is trained to recite to seek absolution for sinning. *Oh my God I am heartily sorry . . .* I repeated again and again, never finishing the rest of the prayer. After nearly five minutes, the shaking stopped. We would find out later the quake was a magnitude 9.2, the strongest ever recorded in North America and still the second strongest quake in the world.

Stunned, we stood silent for a few minutes. Was it really over? Finally, Dad turned back to the house and walked through the open door, still cradling Teri. We had no power. In the dim light of that March evening, the contents of the house had been shaken and put back down like a giant's game of pickup sticks. Chairs, sofa, tables, lamps strewn across the floor. Pictures tossed and shattered. Broken dishes, plants, and dirt covered our special crab dinner. Cupboard doors and drawers ajar. Dad pulled a flashlight out of his tool drawer, handed Teri to Mom, and went outside to inspect the exterior of the house. "Get a broom and start sweeping up the glass," Mom ordered me, "before we step on it and cut ourselves."

By the time I finished sweeping all the glass and dishes into a pile, Dad had returned from his exterior inspection. "No oil leaks, no power lines down in the alley, no large cracks in the house. Bundle up and try to stay warm. I've got to get to the plant." He grabbed a jacket and left. It would be another five days before we saw him again.

That first night, after clearing a safe path to the bedroom, we crowded into Mom's and Dad's bed and tried to sleep. Just as Teri, Patti, Mom, and I snuggled into the warmth of each other's bodies, an aftershock hit. We jumped up, Mom grabbing Teri and heading out the door again. This repeated throughout that first long night. We learned later that in the first twenty-four hours after the initial quake we suffered through eleven aftershocks greater than magnitude 6.2.

Without power, we had no heat and no water. (Even though we had our own well, the pump was powered by electricity.) Phone lines were severed. One radio station stayed on the air and became the de facto emergency operations communication center. We located our only battery-powered radio and listened sporadically, trying to conserve the batteries. The news only traumatized us more. We learned both of our highways, one going north and the other south, were closed by landslides, collapsed bridges, or road beds either risen or sunken. Fourth Avenue, the main street in downtown Anchorage, collapsed, toppling some buildings completely, partially burying others.

When it was light enough to see, Mom, Patty, and I, bundled up in coats, hats, and boots, cleaned up the mess we had missed in the dark the night before, while Teri, in a snowsuit, sat in her playpen.

With the jolt of every aftershock, I was poised to rush out the door, trembling in anticipation of the next one. Mom's anxiety only magnified mine. "How did Paul get to the plant? When will he get back? How will I let my family know I'm okay?" She repeated again and again. She did not know what to do, and I didn't know how to help her. No car, no information, no communication, and no way of knowing when or if things would return to normal.

Fortunately, later that first day, Judy arrived at our front door. "My mom says you should come stay with us. We have heat from our propane kitchen stove, and we can cook."

What relief. With help from Judy, and her sister Kathy and brother Jess, we packed up sleeping bags and air mattresses, the slowly thawing food from our freezer, and Teri's playpen, then marched to the Edge family's house two doors away. Mr. Edge was not at home during the quake. He worked as a carpenter at remote locations around Alaska and was rarely with his family, leaving Mrs. Edge essentially a single mother. She knew how to survive on her own, having already raised seven children, four older ones now living independently out of state, and the three youngest, still living at home.

In those first days after the quake, six kids and two mothers crammed into a house no bigger than our own, sharing food, heat, batteries, radios, and emotional comfort. Schools were closed, some of them destroyed or so badly damaged they could not open until the following year. We did not know when or if our school would be safe enough to reopen.

Though nighttime temperatures were still well below freezing, days rose into the upper thirties. The spring freeze/thaw had begun. Younger kids played outside, making snowballs and snowmen with the sticky wet new snow that fell in the night. Judy and I wandered the neighborhood surveying the damage. The corner store and bowling alley were closed, broken windows boarded up. When we met up with friends we shared stories, telling each other over and over again what had happened and what we had done while the ground was shaking. The more intense aftershocks sent us scrambling home to find out if our houses were still standing. Adults visited each other as they cleaned up debris and shared food, sometimes using fish smokers, fireplaces, or camp stoves to cook. In addition to reporting the extent of damage, the radio station began providing messages to reconnect people—"John Wilson, your wife and kids are safe at Providence Hospital," or "Mary Thomas, Grandma has your kids at her house . . ."

Gradually we gleaned that our misfortunes were small compared to others around the state. A tsunami had inundated Kodiak, Valdez, and Seward, and wiped out the villages of Chenega and Afognak completely, carrying away most of the inhabitants. A fire broke out at the fuel depot at the port of Seward and destroyed what town the tsunami had not already wiped out.

The world could tumble apart at any moment, and I would have no control over anything.

The military stepped in to help during those first few days and for months afterward. The tower at the Anchorage International Airport had collapsed and the airport terminal was structurally damaged, so most of the flights in and out of Anchorage used the field on the air force base. The military flew in food, medical supplies, and materials for repairing roads and bridges. The military even set up food and water distribution centers because most food was shipped to Alaska by air, and with the transportation chain broken, grocery stores had no supplies. Later, immunization centers were set up, offering free shots to prevent the spread of water-borne diseases since both city water and personal wells were thought to be contaminated. Judy's mom must have taken advantage of the supplies offered from the closest government food and water centers. People lined up to fill their cars with cans of food, military rations, and water to bring back home.

Five days after the big quake, power returned to our part of town. Dad had worked day and night with his crew at the military power plant, in conjunction with his colleagues at the city plant, to repair the structural and mechanical damage to the buildings, turbines, and other equipment. At the same time, linemen patched up the severed lines, a massive team effort. When Dad finally came home, he smelled of sweat and badly needed a shave. His eyes were puffy and his clothes filthy. He took a long shower while Mom fixed him a sandwich and handed him a beer.

"It's like a war," he said, "I don't know how we'll ever recover." He ran his finger along the bottom of his empty beer mug and told us the stories of what he had seen. An apartment building shaken apart like a sandcastle. A downtown store and movie theater toppled like a tower of wooden blocks. And in the rich people's neighborhood of Turnagain-by-the-Sea, near the old rabbit hutches, whole houses and people swallowed by the earth. But with Dad at home, I felt like we would be okay, though I never lost my instinct to bolt for the door at the slightest tremor beneath my feet.

From seventh through tenth grade, I flourished in the small Catholic school with its close-knit community of just a few hundred students and its emphasis on academics. My teachers encouraged my college ambitions, and I earned mostly good grades (though I was never good in math). I played clarinet in the school band and joined the intramural basketball team. My father still believed college was not necessary for girls and my mother offered neither encouragement nor discouragement for my dreams. She did not take my side, yet was never as strongly opposed as Dad. She herself had just a high school education and had worked at the airplane factory near Buffalo during the war as a "Rosie the Riveter" and, for few months, as a secretary. But economic independence was out of the norm for women of her generation. After the war, Mom and the other "Rosies" gave up their jobs so men returning from the war could move back into the workforce. Mom seemed content in her role as a mother and homemaker. Though she handled all the family bills, she saw her job as raising kids and managing the household, and had no real economic power in the family. She relied on my dad to earn the money, make the major decisions, and drive her anyplace she couldn't reach on foot or by bus. I did not want that life. I wanted to make my own decisions and earn my own money.

I decided the only way to attend college was by working part-time and summer jobs. Beginning in fifth grade I had started babysitting for neighborhood kids after school and on weekends. Later, from sixth grade through early middle school, I took on full-time summer childcare jobs, making about fifty cents an hour. I saved most of what I earned and when a new movie theater opened in Anchorage I got a job in the concession stand, making about $1.50 an hour. During the summer of my senior year, I worked for the advertising department of the *Anchorage Times*, (one of two city newspapers) delivering tear sheets (copies of ads) to businesses advertising in the paper. I drove a Volkswagen bug from business to business so they could proof upcoming ad copy to appear in the paper. I made a whopping $2.10 an hour, plus learned to drive a standard transmission car.

At that time Alaska had only one university, in Fairbanks, with its extreme cold and winter darkness. I knew I did not want to live in Fairbanks. A small community college existed in Anchorage, but it was geared toward vocational education. I longed to visit the "Outside," which is what we called the rest of the United States. With most of our extended family in the Northeast, I had seen that part of the country and some of Alaska, but nothing in between. What would I find in the bigger world?

Despite the fundraising efforts of parents and parish, as well as a modest tuition charged for each student, our Catholic school ran out of funds at the close of my sophomore year of high school. The next school year, I entered my local public high school, with a population five times the size of the private school. Overwhelmed by the number of students and the choices at my new school, one person eased my transition and brought with him a new set of friends. That person would one day become my husband. His name was Ron. He kept showing up at my locker in between classes or next to me at assemblies. I was flattered by his attention at a time when I was starting over in an unfamiliar and overwhelming environment. His affection was a sign I could fit in at my new school and slip into a ready-made social group. I belonged to someone, and his group of friends took me in. We enjoyed the same things—hiking, sledding, basketball games, movies, and cruising on weekends in someone's father's car. With school, work, and my new social life, I spent less and less time at home.

Chapter Five

A few months after school began, on a Friday in-service day and before my shift at the movie theater started, Dad invited me on a tour of his power plant. Not a public tour, he said, just the two of us, a private take-your-daughter-to-work day. He wanted me to see what he did all day at the power plant. Was he sensing my efforts to pull away from the family? Did he want to strengthen the bond between us? Did he hope I would recognize the importance of his work?

I knew he ran the maintenance department and supervised a crew that kept the turbines and the other machinery running to provide power to the base and the Air Force hospital. That did not tell me what he actually did, though, and I didn't really want to go. I was embarrassed, not wanting to feel like Daddy's little girl in a workplace comprised of only men (except for the plant secretary). But I didn't want to hurt his feelings, so I said yes.

At the base entrance gate, a good-looking young soldier saluted Dad and waved us through. I was surprised Dad was treated like an officer even though he was clearly a civilian. We passed the rows of identical housing units, all painted beige, each with its own steps and tiny porch. We parked behind the plant, a square gray building with chimneys poking high into the sky. Dad opened a door with the jingling mass of keys hooked to his belt and we entered a corridor lined with pipes. The linoleum floors were spotless, gleaming with a shine my mother never achieved on our kitchen floor. In fact, the whole place was cleaner than our house had ever been. Dad introduced me to the men we passed, dressed in the same drab olive-green clothes he wore to work every day.

"This is my daughter," he yelled over the rumble of machines. The men smiled and shook my hand like I was a visiting dignitary. We climbed a set of metal stairs leading to a catwalk with a view of the turbine room. Dad's lips moved, but the noise was so loud I couldn't hear anything he said. I understood now why we had to say things to him more than once. It was a wonder he could hear at all.

He's proud of me, I thought. I should feel honored, allowed entrance into his world of men and machines. I knew his work was important, and his men treated him with respect. But what did any of it have to do with what I wanted: to get out of Alaska, to be on my own? To do what, though, I didn't know.

Dad frequently freelanced electrical work to earn extra money. Not long after the plant tour, he asked me to help him wire a friend's cabin-under-construction. (I agreed to help, not because I wanted to, but, once again, because he wanted me to.)

We drove a couple of hours out of town, then along a boggy road to a cabin on a lake. From his station wagon, Dad unloaded his tools, a spool of black wire, rolls of black tape, lots of little yellow plastic caps, square gray metal electrical boxes open on one side, a battery-powered drill, the thermos of coffee and sandwiches Mom fixed for us, and the beers he brought for himself. Our commotion echoed across the still lake. A pair of grebes called out their raspy complaints. Thin plates of ice clung to shore where the lake was beginning to freeze at night, Fall in Alaska: freezing nights, warm days when the sky was clear. The sharp tang of ripe highbush cranberries pierced the air.

I had taken the day off work to help him. It was a perfect fall day for hiking, which my boyfriend and our group of friends were doing at that moment. I pictured them crammed into Ron's car, driving to the end of the switch-backed road, then hiking into the Chugach Mountains. Instead, I was crawling around in the shell of some stranger's cabin.

Dad flipped his cigarette butt into the lake, and we got started. Inside, the building seemed colder than outside. It smelled like damp wood. Whistling, Dad got to work, drilling holes in the studs, pointing to where I was supposed to thread the black-coated copper wire.

It was a day like this one, he reminded me, when his buddy flew him to a lake that had no road access to it to help build a different cabin. The guy flew back to town for another load of lumber, but the weather socked in, so Dad had to spend the night alone in the outhouse. "A new one," he said, "fortunately." I pictured him hunkered against the wall, smoking, his legs propped over the toilet seat, rain pummeling the roof, with no idea when he would get out.

My fingers stiffened as I fumbled with the wire in the cold. I jabbed my hands with the sharp ends and broke most of my fingernails. As a little girl I was disgusted yet fascinated by Dad's hands—cracked and creased with dirt that wouldn't wash out even with the hard, gritty soap he used. His right forefinger bore a ridged scar down its entire length, the nail split and grown like a claw over his mangled fingertip. It had been smashed beneath the tines of a forklift when he was helping the driver deliver electrical equipment to the plant. In spite of this and other scars, Dad's thick fingers worked with precision—drilling, inserting gray outlet boxes between the studs, attaching them with his battery-operated screwdriver.

He handed me the screwdriver. It took five or six tries for me to line up each screw with the tip of the screwdriver and twirl it into place. Some stuck out into the box and he had to redo them completely. I was a failure as an electrical assistant, long before it was possible for women to even enter the profession. But he said nothing. Maybe all he wanted was my company.

I bounced up and down to warm my toes. Outside, the sun warmed the air and melted the autumn frost. Inside the cabin, last night's chill still clung to the bare walls and floor. By the time we stopped for lunch, I could barely move my bony fingers, and my pencil-thin arms were rubbery from reaching over my head to push wire through studs.

As we sat outside on the steps in the sun, eating our salami sandwiches, Dad said, "Thanks for helping me today, Susie."

"Sure," I said, but what I thought was *I'm never doing this again* and *I will never be the son he wanted.*

***

At the start of my senior year of high school, Ron, a year older, left to attend college at the University of Washington in Seattle. I was free to date other people, but I was so dependent on him I simply kept writing him letters saying how desperately I missed him. I did not want to live my mother's life, but still operated under the culture's expectations of women at that time. You fell in love. If that was the "right person" for you, you married him, had children, and lived happily ever after. Except I wanted what seemed impossible at the time—love *and* independence. I had no idea how to achieve both. I also had no idea what I wanted to do with a college degree.

During my last two years of high school, I earned credits by working in the school library. The head librarian, a curmudgeon named Mr. Crouch, taught the only creative writing course offered on campus. Though he was dour and sarcastic, rarely giving encouragement, he taught us how to *just write*, experiment with genres and styles, read our work, and critique each other. I believed any positive feedback from Mr. Crouch was a sign of true success. From his class, my love of literature and writing took shape and I developed a lifelong love of literature as well as a desire to write.

I applied to only one college, Seattle University, a small Catholic college in inner-city Seattle. My goal was to get away from Alaska but also move closer to Ron. I did not have the money to visit Seattle University's campus beforehand, nor did my parents see the need. I only had the descriptions and pictures in the brochures the university sent me. It seemed a lot like my old Catholic school and its small size felt familiar and safe.

I was surprised and thrilled when the college accepted me. Throughout my senior year I applied for grants and loans. I don't remember any help from my guidance counselor, and certainly none from my family other than providing a financial statement for financial aid. Ironically, all of my requests for funding were denied because my family was not poor enough. The years of living paycheck to paycheck, of running low on groceries at the end of the month, of driving used cars, and I discovered Dad made too much money for me to receive financial aid. Maybe if I had had a better high school counselor or someone who had been to college and knew how to guide me, I could have tapped into resources I knew nothing about.

With careful calculation, I figured I had enough money saved for my first year. (I did not plan beyond that year.) But when the first tuition payment came due, I was $400 short. This new obstacle appeared insurmountable since my job at the newspaper paid less than $3.00 an hour, and time was running out to add another job to my already full-time schedule. I was furious at Dad for making more money than I assumed. Where did it go? *Alcohol*, I thought. But I found out later my parents must have been saving for the new house they bought the year I left for college.

Though Dad was the target of my anger, I did not express my frustration and disappointment to him. Instead, I took my anger out on my mother. "Now I will have to stay home another year and work," I whined. It was unfair.

"You'll get lost in that big city," she said. "You won't make it on your own. You don't even know how to do your own laundry." The more I pulled away, the more my mother tried to wrench me back.

"What do you know?" I countered. "You stayed at home until you got married."

Mom saw no need for education, travel, or current events. I viewed her life as a cage—small, safe, but stifling—from which I needed to escape. I shouted, slammed doors, cried in my room, half-sure she was right. I couldn't make it on my own. Maybe she was worried about the world I was about to enter, far from the isolated and insulated life in Alaska.

One evening toward the end of summer, Dad picked me up from my job at the local newspaper and handed me an envelope. I opened it. Inside were four hundred-dollar bills. I had never held that much cash in my hands before.

Instead of saying, "Thank you," I said, "Where did you get this?"

"Never mind," he said. "Take it."

Did he borrow it? Sell something? Win it playing poker? I didn't care. I kept it. That was the only money he gave me for college, and he never told me where he'd gotten it.

I completed my first year of college, then married Ron, my high school sweetheart, and switched from my small Catholic college to join him at the University of Washington, where I could now qualify for in-state tuition. I found a way, I believed, to have it all—education, marriage, and independence. We pooled our resources, and with summer jobs and frugality, put ourselves through college.

The University of Washington campus had nearly eight times as many students as my tiny Catholic university. UW was a city unto itself, nearly as large as my hometown. Back in Alaska, the "Outside"—the rest of the world—seemed far away. What I knew about it came from television and newspapers. The politics of the rest of the country didn't seem to have much to do with where we lived. At UW, that "Outside" world was all around me. The university offered courses in areas I did not even know existed—black studies, women's studies, Irish history, and others.

At first, I knew no one there except Ron. Since he was a year ahead of me, he guided me through the registration process and helped me locate my classes, but I was on my own in charting a path through the diversity of students, professors, ideas, and disciplines a large university had to offer. Once I got over my intimidation, I took advantage of the rich milieu.

It was the 1960s. The campus was a microcosm of the upheaval in the world around us. Vietnam war protests, campus strikes, walkouts, bullhorns and speeches in the commons. I would arrive at class ready for a lecture only to find out my professor supported the student strike and never showed up. Other times, another instructor might begin class only to be booed and jeered into stopping by protesting students. It was chaotic, confusing, and exhilarating for a girl from small-town Alaska.

I decided to major in Communications, an umbrella degree that included journalism—both broadcast and print—public relations, and advertising. The academic program required a survey of all these components, plus encouraged a wide selection of electives since, if we were going to write about the world and influence opinion, we needed knowledge on a breadth of topics. After my experience in Mr. Crouch's high school class, I only knew I wanted to write. I had no concrete plans for how I could turn an aspiration into a vocation.

Ron and I had met when I was sixteen and he was seventeen. We married at nineteen and twenty. Neither of us had really dated anyone else. When I arrived at the UW campus wearing my wedding ring, I felt as if I were pretending to be a grownup. When other students got together after class or invited me to a party, I always declined. Though I told myself I did not want to live my mother's life, I fell into a familiar role. We were both full-time students, but I did all the cooking and cleaning. As I vacuumed and scrubbed our studio apartment, Ron sat reading or watching television. *Why doesn't he offer to help?* I thought, but only confronted him after my resentment built up over weeks of frustration and I exploded into angry tears. In our tiny apartment, Ron liked to study while watching TV. I needed quiet to concentrate, so I either closed myself in our tiny bathroom to study or walked two miles to the university library or campus center. Without realizing it, I put Ron's needs ahead of my own. His studies were more important than mine. In my first women's studies class, as we introduced ourselves to the other students, I remember saying even though I wanted a career, my husband and family would always come first.

By the end of that course, my beliefs about gender roles had shifted dramatically. I pushed back on handling all the cooking and cleaning, and subordinating my studies to his. I questioned my assumption that I would have children, or that I would stay married forever. My creative writing professor (for whom I nurtured a secret crush) even challenged the whole notion of monogamy. Students of color in my black studies class shredded my disbelief in the existence of structural inequality. Beliefs about myself and the world were slowly cracking, as if by a thousand tiny earthquakes, and settling into a whole new configuration. I quit going to Mass. There were too many discrepancies between church doctrine and the real-life needs of human beings. I still clung to one value I learned from the nuns, though—care for others and care for your community. Ron and I volunteered in a university program to earn credits while tutoring youth in inner city schools. Additionally, I worked in a day care center in the same community.

Though protests against the Vietnam War continued on our campus, and on campuses around the country (sometimes becoming violent as in the Kent State killings in 1970), student strikes at UW subsided and classes resumed.

Ron graduated a year before I did but decided to continue his studies to earn an MBA. We both wanted to settle back in Alaska but dreamed of seeing the country that lay between the west and east coasts before settling down. Ron's parents were planning to retire soon and wanted to buy a truck and trailer to travel around Alaska and the Lower 48. Ron convinced them to make their purchase early and allow us to drive their retirement dream around the country before returning it to them in Alaska. So, with a truck and trailer, and a grant Ron had received to complete a study of consumer credit rates in Washington and Oregon, we began a year-long journey. First we traveled to credit companies in those two states, collecting data on car and other small loans, then, while he analyzed his data and wrote his thesis, we continued down the west coast, across the southwest—taking time to hike down and back up the Grand Canyon—then into Mexico, up through the Southeast, to New York to visit my mother's family, Kansas and Missouri to visit Ron's mother's family, and back across the northern borders of Wyoming, the Dakotas and Canada.

We saw for ourselves the vast landscape we had grown up to simply call the "Outside," and finally, yearning for home, we found our way back to Alaska.

During our long drive around the country, we had plenty of time to talk about children. Ron was sure he wanted children—two or three. He was an only child, having spent a lot of time alone while his parents ran a business, and had always longed for a sibling. I wasn't so sure. I was determined to have a career, but wasn't sure which one, and was also afraid I was too impatient to make a good mother. Also, while other women effused about new babies, I didn't enjoy them. *How was I supposed to act around them?* I sometimes thought. *They seemed so fragile. What if I did something wrong?* Even though my mother had a baby when I was fifteen, and I had plenty of experience babysitting, the thought of being responsible for another human for most of my life filled me with doubts and anxiety.

After returning to Anchorage, Ron and I concentrated on settling down, finding jobs, and getting out of his parents' home where we lived while saving money for our own place. I applied for jobs as a reporter with the newspaper, but there were no openings. I also applied at a local advertising agency but failed their writing test; apparently, I was not quick or witty enough to write ads for them. Wanting to move out of my in-laws home as quickly as possible, I took a job working retail at a furniture store and eventually advanced to customer service. I was ashamed my college education had led to a dead-end job I could have snagged right out of high school.

Chapter Six

The discovery of oil above the Arctic Circle on the North Slope in 1968 led to the construction planning for the oil pipeline from Prudhoe Bay to the port of Valdez, plans which were quickly stalled by lawsuits from environmental groups and Alaska Native tribes. However, this did not stop the rumors about the jobs and cash that would flow into the state once the construction started. Alaska was on the cusp of what would become the biggest boom in its history, and the flow of job seekers became a flood. With a lack of adequate social and health services to meet the needs of people arriving in the state (most with no money and no medical care), an energetic young couple opened a free clinic, called Open Door Clinic, staffed by volunteer doctors and a few paid medical and counseling staff. Frustrated with my job answering complaints about late furniture deliveries, I volunteered at the clinic, answering crisis calls and referring people to services, all while learning what it meant to be poor in my hometown. I found I enjoyed working with the clients, and felt I was contributing something to solve the social problems in my rapidly growing community. The staff, who had mostly come to Alaska from other places in the country, were young, adventurous, and ambitious, seeking to launch careers in a place where their skills were desperately needed. Eventually, the director invited me to join the paid staff, working for the nurse as a medical assistant and counselor. I accepted, setting aside my writing ambitions to work as part of a team of altruistic young people.

Ron and I had been married seven years by then. He was ready to start a family. I was venturing into a new kind of work. I wanted to be sure, but I was already twenty-six years old; some of my peers were already having their second children. Would I ever be sure? Would there ever be a better time? But, beneath that, something deeper: memories of that five-year-old bringing coffee to a bedridden mother, the eight-year-old sobbing on Dad's shoulder, the teenager overhearing her mother making one more try for a healthy baby. I feared giving birth to dead babies, but I told myself I was not my mother. Medical care was much better than in my mother's generation. What was I waiting for? In my work at the clinic, I saw plenty of women having babies without the agonizing decision-making process I was going through.

Once our daughter Elisha was born, I fell in love with her. Blond hair, blue eyes, and fair skin, she took after her father's side of the family and, since he was an only child, his parents showered their one grandchild with attention and gifts. (I'm sure my parents loved her equally, but as the second of their grandchildren, they were less extravagant with her.)

After a few weeks of maternity leave I went back to work part-time at the clinic, leaving Elisha with my mother. I enjoyed helping people, but there was so much I didn't know. Our clients, mostly young and poor, arrived at our doorstep with the gamut of problems: pregnancy, sexually transmitted diseases, drug addiction, mental health crises, homelessness. I could listen and recommend resources, but what more could I do? I didn't know how to help people recover from trauma, or make healthier choices in their lives, or find ways out of addiction and domestic violence. Surely there was a body of knowledge to help me understand people's psychological pain, and techniques and strategies to help them move forward.

Shortly after Elisha was born, I decided to enter a graduate program in counseling psychology at the University of Alaska Anchorage. With Ron's promotion at the bank (where he had embarked on a successful career in IT) and my mom providing childcare, I quit work and attended school full time.

Since returning to Alaska and moving out of our parents' homes, we had been living in a two-bedroom apartment in Spenard, though we dreamed of building our own house. Ron, before changing his university major to quantitative methods, started out in the field of architecture, and had worked for a drafting firm during high school. He drew up our preliminary house plans. Throughout my pregnancy we searched for property in the foothills of the Chugach Mountains above Anchorage. We found a half-acre lot on a dirt road with a panoramic view of the city and Cook Inlet. There were only two other houses on our road at that time, and we would be within walking distance of Chugach State Park, a half-million-acre wilderness. Reaching our house would require a four-wheel drive vehicle in winter, but we already had a four-wheel drive pick-up truck as well as a small sedan.

When Elisha was barely two, we began work on the house, hiring a contractor for foundation and framing, and calling on family help for other crucial elements. Ron worked with his dad, who had his own contracting business, to install the plumbing and heating, and with my father to install the electrical system. Our construction project strained Ron's relationship with his father, who was frequently impatient and critical of him, and Ron worked more easily with my father. Neither one was a great talker, so they worked quietly side-by-side, Ron following Dad's instructions and catching on quickly. "Here," Dad told me later, with pride and surprise, "was a college boy who could work with his hands."

My role throughout this phase of construction was to keep our toddler busy and out of harm's way, feed whatever crew was working, haul in materials, and haul out debris. We moved into the house while it was still a shell, with only studs for walls and bare floors. We continued working nights and weekends to finish the interior and achieve what we believed would be our dream home.

While in graduate school I started working at a family counseling center. Ron and I had been married ten years by then, and with the stress of school, my new career, parenting, and continual work on our house, fissures began to appear in our relationship. At the same time I had begun forming new friendships with my fellow graduate students. Unlike when I was an undergraduate, I sometimes joined them for parties, after-class discussions, and hikes. Likewise, Ron periodically joined his co-workers at a local bar after work to play pool, returning home smelling like beer long after I went to bed. If we were not talking about our home construction or our daughter, we had little to discuss besides who was staying out too late. We did less and less together, and I found myself regretting getting married so young, before I had had a chance to live on my own as an adult.

In my graduate program, we explored the psychological and social issues I had observed at my job at Open Door Clinic, and we were required to examine our own backgrounds, relationships, and significant events in our lives, reflecting on how they would influence our ability to help others. We demonstrated the techniques we were learning in mock counseling sessions, critiqued each other, and were graded on our performances. I was frightened and intimidated at first, but the more I practiced, the more confident I became in my counseling abilities, and also in myself. To relieve stress and peel off some of my remaining pregnancy fat, I began running along the switch-back roads of our new mountainside neighborhood, and into the forests and tundra of the nearby state park. A neighbor joined me with her Irish Wolfhound, Bear, as tall as my waist. With two of us and her dog, we felt confident in fending off any real bears we might encounter.

"Be careful," she told me once, as my running stamina increased. "Someday you might run right out of your marriage."

At the same time the gap between Ron and me widened, my relationship with Dad also deteriorated. One Sunday, Mom invited Ron, Elisha, and me to dinner. Dad greeted me with a hug and lifted his granddaughter up to plant a raspberry on her neck. She giggled and wrapped her arms around him.

I pulled her away. He radiated a sickening fusion of aftershave and whiskey and was *way* too happy. A familiar twinge of dread and shame seized my gut. I didn't want to watch him stumble and slur his words or have my daughter witness this. I was embarrassed and angry at him, and ashamed of Mom for putting up with it. She was totally dependent on him for everything. Standing at the door with Elisha in my arms, I tried to fabricate an excuse to flee—headache, nausea, a pot left on the stove. But I looked at all the work Mom had put into the meal and lost my resolve.

When we sat down for a dinner of pot roast, green beans, and potatoes, Dad downed too many glasses of cheap red wine from a big glass jug, had stopped eating, sat back in his chair, and said nothing as the rest of us continued eating. His face was flushed and his eyes red. I felt sad and embarrassed to see him this way. Mom ignored him, and turned her conversation to my little sister, Teri, who still lived at home but was spending the night with a friend.

Mom complained that Teri had little interest in school, but they wanted her to go to college.

"Wait," I said. "I wanted to go to college, but you didn't help me at all."

I went on about how they were spoiling my sister, about all the things she had I never had, the things she could do I never could. The typical complaints of an oldest child.

Without warning, Dad stood, staggered from his chair, and started yelling. "You think you're so smart with all your college. I'm sick of hearing about it. Quit looking down on everyone else."

Ron stared at the table in silence while Elisha climbed into her grandma's lap. I forgot all the accumulated successes of my adult life, and at that moment became the little girl who somehow made Daddy angry. Mom apologized and begged us to stay, but I scooped up my daughter, grabbed my husband and, like a coward, escaped.

Chapter Seven

A deep brown Alaska lake lined with thick, silky muck. A spindly forest of spruce, willow, and alder. A swamp of bog blueberry, cinquefoil, cotton grass, and sweet-scented Labrador tea. Mosquitoes, fierce and dense. Trout and salmon. Loons, ducks, grebes, gulls. Beaver, muskrat, moose, and bears. Berries. Once, a place of Dena'ina fish camps and villages, hunters and trappers. Once, a place of plenty.

On a map, lines are drawn, long thin rectangles, each with a slice of ragged lakeshore. Little strips of land sold at a tidy profit. One went to my father.

Early in June 1977, the ground still thawing, I steered the old Dodge through slimy mud, around yawning potholes, along a maze of roads crudely cut through the trees. Driveways plowed through gangly black spruce, alder, and willow. The lots all looked alike. At last, at the base of a long, steep driveway, I spotted Dad's red pickup truck parked next to a mustard-colored cabin perched on short concrete columns. A ragged bulge like an old scar ran along the roof line.

Dad popped his head out the back door, his black hair sticking out from under his gold-braided captain's hat and his blue, zippered overalls stretched taut across his belly. As I opened my door, a floatplane roared across the water. In a flash of red, it lifted and took off.

"You found us," Dad yelled over the deafening noise of the plane.

"It wasn't hard," I lied.

"I'll show you around." He waved me forward. "Crappy color," he said, indicating the new-to-him cabin. "I'm gonna paint it."

Mom and Dad had been camping at Nancy Lake for decades, first with a tent and later in their small motorhome. About seventy miles north of Anchorage, they could easily reach it in a little more than an hour. Much of the shoreline was private property, but a large portion belonged to the state, designated for recreational use, including a small campground and boat launch accessible by road, and two public-use rental cabins reached by foot, boat, skis, or snowmobiles. The lake is deceptively large, with hidden coves, inlets, and outlets to explore. Dad fished from a canoe and Mom picked berries in the fall. They fell in love with the quiet beauty of the water, the cry of loons, the dense forest. With Dad's retirement income from his government job and his new job as Director of Maintenance at Providence Hospital, they were able to buy their retirement dream.

On the day I visited their "new" cabin, none of that peace and serenity was apparent. A pack of jet skis streaked across the water, filling the space where the plane had been. Seconds later, the wake hit the dock and sent it kicking and screeching against its metal moorings.

"They joined two cabins together." Dad pointed to the roof. "Two for the price of one. Might have to jack it up here or there."

That would mean regular maintenance. When you build on a swamp, a cabin will heave and buckle in freeze and thaw. As Dad escorted me to the property line, we sank to our ankles in ground as springy as foam rubber. We didn't have to go far. Faded orange survey tape drooped from weathered wooden stakes a few paces from each side of the cabin.

"These lots are close," I said.

"But we're right on the lake."

In order to maximize their profits by cramming as many lake front lots as possible onto the properties, subdividers created narrow strips of land with long driveways down to the lake. This meant, though cabins crowded close to the shore, the property stretched in a long ribbon from the access road.

"Is it always this noisy?"

"Only on the weekends."

A sliver of land. The din of water sports. A rugged shack. A tilting outhouse. This would be my inheritance.

"Not bad," was all I said.

Dad battled the alders, burning fresh saplings with a blow torch. Not overly effective since they spread by their roots, but he had a smile on his face. He was outside, busy, working with his hands.

Neighbors multiplied nearly as fast as the alders. A gnarled old railroad worker and his clan bought two lots on the north side of Mom and Dad's land. They rented a small bulldozer and cleared the land from road to lake, built a two-story cabin, then hauled in several sheds, dug a massive fire pit near the water, and threw a roof over it. The thin line of surviving trees on Dad's property barely veiled the snowmobiles, boats, four-wheelers, pickup trucks, campers, and various parts dumped on their land. The owners reveled in all-night drunken parties around a campfire.

"I'd like to shoot them," Dad complained.

Dad's former coworker bought the lot on the other side of the cabin. He razed the few trees left between his lot and my parents', creating a straight shot for snowmobiles that raced from the road to the lake in winter. When Mom brewed her morning coffee she looked directly into this neighbor's window.

My parents added their own clutter to the neighborhood—a tool shed, a greenhouse, a speedboat, water skis, a bright red canoe, an aluminum row boat. The sliver of land stretching beside the long driveway allowed ample room for the accumulation of toys. Joining the winter uproar on the ice, Dad bought his own snowmobile. Mom, though she was shy, enjoyed having company and welcomed the visitors all these new possessions attracted.

I wanted nothing to do with the place. The lots carved from the lakeshore reminded me of the trailer court I used to cut through on my way to elementary school. Close. Rackety. Stinking of swamp with a tinge of sewage. Neither did the cabin itself hold any attraction: one bedroom, a kitchen/living/sleeping room, no running water, no electricity, and an outhouse that would fill with ground water in the spring and during heavy rains.

Rather than visit, Ron, Elisha, and I most often sped past the turn-off to Dad's slice of paradise. I couldn't understand what happened to the man I knew as a kid, the one who took us to wild places where we could run free without banging into other people.

But Alaska was changing and so was Dad. He'd quit smoking—again—but he sometimes started drinking at lunch and kept at it until nodding off in the recliner at night. I couldn't predict the phase of drunkenness he might be in when we'd visit—happy, sentimental, pissed-off, apathetic, or conked out. I didn't want to witness any of it, nor did I want my daughter to see him like that.

But she begged. "Please, Mom. I want to roast marshmallows and drive Grandpa's boat. We could go swimming."

So, every now and then we made a day of it. A long-time birder, I'd bring my binoculars and scout for waterfowl on the lake and shorebirds in the swamp (if we arrived before the water sports sent all the wildlife diving for cover). We packed a picnic, paddled the canoe, dove off the dock if the weather was hot, let Dad give us a tour of the lake in his speedboat, made ourselves sick on s'mores, and came home late, dirty and stinking of campfire smoke, everyone happy but me.

A house, a history, and a child were not enough to sustain my marriage to Ron. We had been Alaskan kids anxious to leave our parents' homes and explore the world Outside. We had grown into adults with different interests and goals and not much to talk about anymore. Ron continued his work running the IT department at the bank and I worked as a family therapist for a nonprofit counseling center. He was content to stay home, watch TV, and work on our never-finished home, while I belonged to a women's group and was teaching parenting workshops in addition to working with troubled families. On weekends I went hiking or running to help relieve the stress of my job.

When I told my parents Ron and I were divorcing my dad said, "After all that work to build your house, why would you get a divorce now?" I could not explain. I knew Dad blamed me for being selfish. He hated to lose a son-in-law he liked and admired. Mom told me she wasn't surprised. Though I thought we were hiding our problems, she somehow had noticed the growing rift between us, but had never said anything.

Initially Ron and I agreed I would have legal custody of Elisha but he would have regular visitation once a week and every other weekend. But at some point in the divorce process he changed his mind and decided he wanted full custody. Since he was using his parents' business attorney, maybe the man thought custody could be used as a bargaining chip in our financial settlement. Or maybe Ron's parents thought if he didn't have custody, I would keep them from seeing their only granddaughter. Then again, maybe he was simply angry because I initiated the divorce; I never found out what changed his mind. But disputing custody meant a trial, interviews by the court custody investigator, a recommendation, and a final determination by a judge. Fortunately, our financial battles were separated from custody consideration. Since I was a family counselor, I found the questioning by the investigator humiliating both professionally and personally. I knew I was a good parent, but the threat of losing custody of our daughter was terrifying. Ultimately, the judge—biased, I was sure, in favor of mothers keeping their daughters, especially since joint custody was not yet generally accepted back then as a formal legal status —awarded me full custody of Elisha, with generous visitation for Ron.

I was thirty years old, had never lived by myself, or owned a car, or had my own credit card. I had a lot to learn and a lot to feel guilty about. I had taken my daughter away from the father she adored when she had just started kindergarten, and though I kept her in the same school, we moved from a big house to a small apartment in a new neighborhood. I wondered if there would have been a better time to get a divorce, even though I could not imagine living the rest of my life with Ron.

Chapter Eight

During the months of negotiations between my lawyer and Ron's, in a period when Ron and I were no longer living together, I met Jim at the agency where I worked. He was a volunteer and one of my duties was to provide training to new volunteers. Jim and I chatted after one of my workshops, and later he called to ask me for a date. I put him off, saying I only had time every other week when Ron took Elisha for the weekend. He said he'd wait.

Jim was unemployed at the time, working summers as a seasonal fisheries biologist with the Alaska Department of Fish and Game. The job offered no benefits and at the start of each season he had to reapply for a position to work at remote camps around the state. When I met him, he was looking for permanent work that would provide more financial stability. He had himself been divorced a few years earlier but had no children.

For our first date he took me to lunch at one of the most expensive restaurants in town. I thought he was either very frugal to have set aside enough money to splurge on an expensive meal, or a complete spendthrift. But it wasn't the restaurant or the meal that caught my attention. After the pressure of my divorce and custody battle, Jim made me laugh, telling one joke after another, and I was fascinated by the stories of his adventures and calamities working in the wilds of Alaska. And he was curious about me. After what seemed like years of living with Ron's silence, I was hungry for conversation.

Jim was in his second career. He had worked as a photographer to pay for college, and when he completed his degree in ecology, had gotten a job as a photographer for a biological textbook company. When he moved to Alaska with his former wife, a physical therapist with a job waiting for her, he took a humiliating job in retail until he could find work with fish and game as a biologist.

When my divorce was final, I bought a small house in an older working-class neighborhood of Anchorage, far from the heights of the mountain house we had built, and farther still from my old home base in Spenard. Elisha and I settled into the close-knit neighborhood conveniently near her school, bike trails, and a grocery store. Jim eventually landed a new permanent job with the University of Alaska doing fisheries studies for a hydroelectric project to be built on Kodiak Island. He was away at a field camp for weeks at a time, but we continued to see each other when he was in town. During one of those weeks off he planned a fishing trip with his college friend Skip from Colorado and Skip's partner Louise. He invited me to join them. It meant six days rafting the Talachulitna River, a world-famous fly-fishing destination in South-central Alaska. Skip, an avid fly fisherman, had been saving for the trip for years.

Though I had paddled a canoe across lakes on multi-day trips, I had never paddled a raft, nor had I floated a remote river. But with his abundance of raft and wilderness experience, I trusted Jim's expertise. He found a one-stop charter service that would rent rafts and fly us into Judd Lake, at the headwaters of the Tal, and pick us up downriver six days later. I was excited about this new adventure and took a week off work, arranging for my parents to keep Elisha while I was gone.

In Skip's fishing magazines, the Tal ran clear, cold, and fast. Now, in early June after a late spring, we discovered a meaner, dirtier version of the Tal. Trees yanked from the banks at break-up. Mangled limbs, broken logs, chunks of earth and roots, all swirling in the chocolate water.

The pilot helped us unload our gear, most things tucked in waterproof bags. Finally, the men unloaded our two deflated rafts. As the pilot turned to leave, he handed us a pump to inflate the rafts, confirmed our pick-up point, and took off.

I tried not to listen to the ferocity of the river as we divided the gear into two piles, one for each raft. The water was so much more threatening than I had imagined. We took turns pumping air into the first raft with the foot pump. When the tubes were taut, we turned to the next raft. *Huff. Huff. Huff.* It took a lot longer to inflate. Then we noticed a faint hiss. We splashed lake water on the rubber tube, trying to locate the leaking air. An old patch on the outer pontoon gurgled, the source of the leak. We pulled the patch kit from a pocket on the raft. Empty. No glue, no patches, nothing but a bag of cellophane and empty glue tubes left by the last people to rent this raft. Ditto on Skip and Louise's patch kit. Okay, we thought, it seemed to be a slow leak, so we'll just pump it up every time we stop for breaks. Jim and I stashed the pump in our raft, loaded the divided gear into both rafts, strapped everything in, and shoved off into the river.

That first day we successfully avoided slamming into the sweepers—trees toppled from their banks, thrust into the current. Jim and I followed Skip and Louise, more skillful paddlers, imitating their moves and directions. That night we made camp, celebrated with beers, enjoyed a freeze-dried dinner, pumped up the raft, and crashed, exhausted. There was no sense in fishing because the river was too swift and murky.

The next day, back on the river, my body reminded me of how unprepared I was for this journey. I scraped my thumb knuckle—not for the first time—against the side of the raft. The cold water froze the pain for a few seconds before the burn returned. The knot above my right shoulder blade throbbed and my shoulder spasmed.

I paddled from the bow, hip waders pulled all the way up my thighs and cinched securely with rubber straps to the belt at my waist. Straddling the raft's tube, one foot dangled in the water while the other was jammed into the toehold at the bottom of the boat, my butt cheeks wrapped tightly around the slowly deflating rubber pontoon.

Jim was not the expert I thought he was. We were not a paddling team, instead awkwardly careening against snags and boulders, twisting around, heading downriver backwards.

"Paddle deeper," he said. "Quit splashing water on me."

I tried but could not find the rhythm. It did not help that our raft grew more flaccid as the day wore on, victim of the slow leak. In frustration over my own incompetence, I blamed Jim for choosing the wrong company, for failing to check the raft before we left, for not doing a better job of steering this sagging rubber duck. I blamed myself for once again trusting a man more than I trusted myself, for not checking the rental company out myself, for believing if he said he knew something, he did. Maybe I shouldn't have expected a man to take care of me. Maybe I should have learned to take care of myself.

After lunch, the river required even more precision. Skip and Louise bobbed ahead with their robust raft and years of experience. Jim and I conquered a sharp dogleg in the river, and it seemed we were catching on. But dead ahead a spruce tree spanned nearly the entire river, sending most of the flow to a narrow channel river-right. Its tangled branches raked the current, grasping and holding leaves, roots, even the top of someone's lost cooler.

"Back paddle," Jim screamed. "Hard! Goddammit!"

The sluggish raft drifted on, gliding with the river's inevitable flow.

"Paddle! Hard! Hard! Goddammit it! Paddle!"

Pull. Pull. Pull. My puny arms could not withstand the churning current. Like a flushing toilet, the water sucked us toward the spruce until we were caught in its tines. Against the tree, the raft slowly buckled in the surging river.

"Jump!" Jim yelled above the roar. "Get the hell out!"

He was crazy. We were over a hole. It was deep. Five minutes is all you have in water this cold. But something in his voice made me obey. I slipped over the edge and slid into the frigid water. It flooded my nose, scraping my scalp like a blade, stunning my heart. All movement in my limbs ceased as the water whirled me like a chunk of driftwood. Then my cheap yellow life jacket took over and popped my head above the surface. But my water-filled hip waders held me suspended in the river.

This was not how I was going to die.

Near the surface, a fat root protruded from the undercut bank. I kicked my leaden legs and grabbed for the slippery wood. My arms grew fierce and powerful. Hand-over-hand, inch-by-inch, I dragged my body up the base of the tree and heaved one knee onto the bank, then the other. I crawled to a mat of spongy moss and staggered to my feet. Unsnapping the bootstraps from my belt, I peeled the legs down, water gushing out and puddling at my feet.

"Where are you?" Jim yelled from below me.

"Over here."

I leaned out over the bank, one hand clamped to a willow, thinking he was caught in the water. But no. He stood mid-river on the trunk of the tree that now trapped our raft.

"The raft is underwater," he yelled. "You have to walk across the tree."

I didn't respond. My brain was still in shock.

"The raft's pinned under the tree. You have to get to the other side of the river with Skip and Louise."

Hypothermic shivers took over. I stumbled toward Jim's voice and peered into the river at the same log that had claimed the raft minutes ago. I had to grab a branch on the tree holding the raft captive, pull myself onto its trunk, and step around and over the protruding branches to reach the other side. My legs were not capable of this feat.

A great thrashing and crackling occurred below me. In a flash of blue and yellow, Jim leaped from the tree trunk, climbed the riverbank, and grabbed my hand.

"I thought you went under with the raft," he said. "I didn't know where you were."

His eyes were wide. He pulled my soaking body to his chest. The buckles on our life jackets clicked and scraped together.

"Come on. We've got to find our gear."

He gripped my elbow and led me to the bank. Together we climbed onto the spruce that still held our raft under water, threaded our way through its broken branches, and vaulted from the crown of the tree to the opposite bank.

Skip and Louise waited for us on the shore. They avoided our calamity with swift maneuvering around the tree, then, seeing our fate, hauled out of the river. Louise had built a tepee of twigs, grass, and driftwood, and now nurtured a tiny flame.

"Strip," she says. "You've got to warm up."

Calm, sensible, grounded Louise. I sat on a rock while she yanked off my boots. She handed me a pair of her pants and a sweatshirt, and I tugged on their dry warmth. The fire gained heat and I rubbed my hands over the flame. As the blood returned to my brain and extremities, understanding of our predicament sank in. One raft, four people, half the gear, half the food, four more days until our pick-up downstream. As far as we knew, there was no one else on the river.

While I was warming up, Jim and Skip waded downriver to catch gear escaping from the submerged raft. Sleeping bags, pads, day packs, tent. Intact, but wet in their river bags. Finally, after an hour (or was it two?), the power of the current flushed the raft from the teeth of the fallen spruce. Had I not jumped overboard I would have been caught with the raft and drowned.

The men snagged the partially limp raft by the dangling bow line and dragged it to our makeshift camp. We inventoried the supplies from the raft: cookies and crackers turned to mush; freeze dried packets intact; Jim's camera destroyed. We had lost one case of beer—and our only pump. We had no way to reinflate our sagging raft.

Over a pot of macaroni and cheese and fried soggy fig bars, we replayed the disaster again and again. Jim and I accepted equal blame for the inept paddling. As our campfire died, our options dwindled to two: stay put and hope someone came along with a patch kit and pump, or continue downriver in the morning, with hopes of finding help. We decided to transfer most of our remaining gear to Skip's and Louise's raft and keep moving. Though our raft was sagging, without its heavy load we might still get another day or two out of it.

In our tent that night Jim and I kicked off our shoes and slid fully clothed into clammy sleeping bags. Midnight sun filtered through the blue walls of the tent, now nearly dry, casting our skin in a pale somber wash. We drew the nylon bags to our chins.

"I thought you were gone," he said.

"You told me to jump in the river."

"The raft was buckling."

"You saved my life." Amazed at my body's power to survive, I think, *I saved myself.*

"What will we do without a pump?" Jim wondered.

"Fuck the river. I want to go home."

"We could have died," he said.

"Yeah."

He unzipped his sleeping bag, reached over, unzipped mine and pulled my sweatshirt over my head. We took off our clothes and held each other skin to skin, not with passion, but as two survivors seeking comfort from each other.

"I should have checked the raft myself before we left," he said, for maybe the tenth time.

I shouldn't trust you completely, I thought, but didn't say it. I couldn't afford to take these chances, to leave my daughter to be raised by her father. Trust should be given sparingly, sifted carefully through your own good sense and reasoning, not dumped wholesale onto someone else.

"The raft won't have enough air to make it through the rapids at the end of the trip," Jim whispered.

"There have to be other people on the river," I said. "We'll find them."

Not long after the Talachulitna trip, Jim purchased a sturdy orange ocean-going raft with a small motor. We towed the raft 250 miles, Anchorage to Homer, and from there motored about forty-five minutes across Kachemak Bay to a small island. It was high tide when we arrived, making offloading easier without a long haul up the beach. Though our landing point was mostly rock and coarse sand interspersed with clumps of yellow daisy-like flowers called beach fleabane, cliffs towered along the windward side. After we unloaded our gear, Jim motored the raft back out into the water, dropped an anchor, let out a couple hundred feet of rope, came back to shore, tied the rope and attached pulley to a stout spruce, and sent the boat floating back into the water. That way, when the tide went out, the boat would still be floating, not grinding on the rocky bottom. It was a complicated process due to the tide differential (averaging fifteen feet, but often with greater extremes), calculating where to drop the anchor, and how much rope was needed to keep the raft secure, but not high and dry.

That done, we pitched our tents behind the storm berm, the jumble of driftwood, seaweed, and debris deposited during the highest tides of the season. While I puttered around, organizing a beach kitchen, getting ready for dinner, Jim said he had to relieve himself and walked into the bushes.

His recollection of what happened next may well differ from mine. Time passed. I gathered firewood, mixed up our one-pot meal, wrote in my journal, watched a kingfisher skim the water and grab a fish. I waited. And waited. How could a person disappear on a small island? Cliffs on one side, beach on the other, ocean all around. Through grass, over driftwood, into the alders. I scrambled into the brush where I last saw him. Branches slapped my face and my feet tripped over hidden driftwood. No sign of him. No luck. Had it been an hour? Two? More? I backtracked to camp, sweat soaking through my shirt. "Jim!" I yelled until I was hoarse. The wind swept my words away. Still he didn't appear. Had he climbed the cliffs for a better view? I resolved to circumnavigate the island. Searching for—what? Bits of clothing stuck to rocks, a body floating in the water? I could not stop the gruesome images rolling through my brain. The faster my heart beat the more helpless I felt.

I thought of making my way back to the harbor, summoning help there. But I didn't know if I could haul the raft back in or how to start the engine, steer the boat, navigate the waves. I remembered a flare tucked somewhere in the raft. Did this constitute the sort of emergency for which it was intended? Amid my fear and concern, I hated myself for being so dependent on Jim, for not measuring up to the image of the tough self-sufficient Alaskan woman I aspired to be.

At last I heard a faint scuffing, and he emerged from the brush. My fears gave way to fury.

"Where were you?"

"Just checking out the tide pools."

"How could you be gone for so long?"

"It was only a few minutes."

"It was hours!" I shouted. "You left me here by myself!"

"What's the big deal?"

"You only think about yourself."

"You're just overreacting."

At the time, I had no idea how often we would repeat similar scenes in various settings. Again and again, Jim demonstrated an aggravating ability to lose himself in his surroundings. He was still the boy who told his mother he was going to Mass every morning before school but instead detoured through a swamp to search for salamanders and red-winged blackbirds.

This focus, this ability to follow his own curiosity, to pause and appreciate a plant, bird, or the way the sun hits a blade of grass, opened my eyes to beauty and adventures I would never discover on my own, plodding along on the well-trod path, dwelling on what could go wrong. These were the things I loved about Jim. And hated.

Jim didn't want to marry me. Not that he didn't want to be with me, he said, but one failed marriage was enough for him. He had married his college sweetheart, moved to Alaska for her job, then while he worked in the field as a biologist, she fell in love with someone else. They had no children and after seven years of marriage, they divorced. Why take the risk of another failure? Better to leave the door open for a clean exit. We could buy a house, share expenses, share parenting, but marriage was not necessary.

Easy for him to say—he didn't have a young daughter. In her presence, I felt ashamed to introduce the man who shared my house as my boyfriend. It was a matter of dignity—she deserved a proper stepfather—and I wanted a commitment.

After three years of dating and three years of living with Jim, I was ready for the romance of a formal marriage proposal, a proclamation of undying love. Champagne and roses instead of our episodic bickering about the value of the institution of marriage.

"If that's what makes you happy."

That's the proposal I got.

I accepted. A simple wedding with friends and my family, though Jim's family boycotted the event, displeased he had never annulled his first marriage.

Elisha and I had met Jim's parents, Joe and Lucille, on their trip to Alaska before the three of us started living together. We shared dinner one evening at a restaurant, and the next day I took Lucille out to pick cranberries in the woods near our house. I enjoyed my time with her on that warm fall day, but neither one of us talked about my future with her son.

The next time I saw Jim's parents was at their house in Lakewood, Colorado. It was my first visit there. Jim, Elisha, and I had been living together for three years by then. That day Jim and I had been shopping for wedding rings in downtown Denver while Elisha spent the day with Lucille. Later, we crowded around the massive oak table in Lucille and Joe's dining room for dinner with Jim's brother Paul, his wife Carol and daughter Selena. Pot roast, mashed potatoes, gravy, iced tea, and Lucille's home-canned corn and beets. We joined hands as Joe recited the blessing. Nine-year-old Elisha fidgeted, not sure what she should say or do during this unfamiliar ritual. I clasped her warm, soft hand in my sweaty palm, my stomach churning not from hunger, but from dread. Knowing how the family had disapproved of Jim's divorce and his refusal to get an annulment, I feared the worst from Joe—rejection, outrage, tongue-lashing.

When the pot roast was sliced and the food passed, Jim cleared his throat. "We have an announcement to make." Heads turned his way. "We're getting married."

I held up my left hand to show the simple gold band with embedded ruby Jim had placed on my finger earlier in the day.

"Congratulations!" Jim's brother slapped him on the shoulder.

"Well, that's nice," said Lucille.

"A wedding!" Jim's niece Selena applauded.

Joe was silent.

"We haven't set a date yet, but we're thinking of sometime next summer, at home in Alaska." I forced a smile. "You're all invited, of course."

Knives and forks scraped against plates. I chewed slowly, cupping my shaky hands around a sweaty glass of iced tea, watching my brand-new ruby gleam in the harsh overhead light. I hated myself for hoping our news would be greeted with joy, acceptance, and maybe hugs around the table.

"Well, that's just fine," Joe said at last, not attempting to hide his sarcasm. "I'll have some more of that gravy."

I coughed away a lump in my throat as the meal wore on in silence. In Joe's eyes his son and I were sinners, previously married in the Catholic Church to other people. We had no right to get married again. The only route to redemption was an annulment, a process requiring you to swear you had entered your former marriage in bad faith, in effect wiping away the existence of that union. Neither Jim nor I was willing to do that, especially since it meant negating Elisha's legitimacy.

Finally, Lucille rose to clear the table. "Anyone want dessert?" she asked.

"What are we having?" Elisha piped up.

"If you have to ask, you don't deserve any," Joe barked.

What a rude, petty thing to say to a guest in your house, I thought. Elisha turned to me, wondering what she'd done wrong. I rubbed her knee under the table and stared at Jim. He lifted his eyebrows. Lucille slipped her dessert anyway.

A few months later we were married on a rainy day at a park near our home in Alaska. We were surrounded by people we loved and who loved us, including kids running wild, longtime friends, and my family, who trusted Jim's quiet, steady love of their daughter and granddaughter. On the groom's side, no one attended.

Our timing could not have been more unfortunate. Because of a precipitous drop in oil prices, the Alaskan economy was in shambles. Banks were closing, people were losing their houses and businesses and deserting the state. Jim had just begun a new financial planning business, I had just been laid off from my job at the counseling center, and a gigantic house payment loomed over us each month. With little cash to spare, for our honeymoon we rented an unfinished cabin on Kachemak Bay. What made our honeymoon memorable? Not the cabin—snug and watertight, but without interior walls and insulation, the privy hanging over the cove, our cooking done on a camp stove, our drinking water hauled from a nearby creek. No, it was that old canoe, the one we borrowed from the shoreline, paddling around the lagoon, periodically landing to poke around empty cabins and gather treasures the tide had washed up. With one canoe between us, he stuck with me, leaving the impression his meandering days were over. Yet, sometime in the years that followed we committed ourselves to annual treks—*together*—to new destinations in our home state and around the world—Africa, Central America, Cuba, Fiji, Europe—certain we would run out of life before we ran out of adventures.

Chapter Nine

When I entered Dad's hospital room, the tube had been removed from his throat. Sitting up, he tried to smile.

"Can't talk much," he whispered and pointed to his throat before lifting a plastic cup to suck water through a straw. Skin sallow, thick lips cracked. Dried saliva caked the corners of his mouth.

The small-town doctor who took him from the paramedics said Dad had congestive heart failure, a damaged heart with a sluggish pump that allowed fluid to build up and fill his lungs. He had nearly drowned, the doctor said.

Mom and Dad had been spending the weekend at the cabin. Dad complained of a cold and kept taking decongestants in hopes of breathing easier. During the night his breathing became increasingly labored. Mom became alarmed and hurried to the cabin next door, belonging to Dad's co-worker. "Paul can't breathe!" she told him. Before cell phones, and with no land lines in the area and Dad gasping for air, Mom feared she was losing him. Fortunately, the neighbor was an amateur ham radio operator and was able to contact the nearest fire station—twenty miles away—for help. But instead of waiting for the fire department to navigate the labyrinth of roads to the cabin, the neighbor put Mom and Dad in his boat, started up the engine, and sped across the lake to the shore nearest the road. There the paramedics met them, opened up Dad's airway, and transported him to the nearest hospital thirty miles away.

When I, my two sisters, and Jim met Mom at the hospital, the emergency room doctor told us Dad's prognosis was not good. Although he might get better, the chances of a long-term recovery were slim. We didn't want to rely on the expertise of an ER doctor from a small rural hospital, so we decided to have him transferred to the Anchorage hospital where Dad worked, forty-five miles away, to see a heart specialist. Now, under the care of a cardiologist, he was breathing on his own and would begin a cardiac rehab program when he was stronger.

I could have talked to this doctor directly, telling him how much Dad smoked and drank, but I left that to Mom. Instead, I decided to confront Dad directly about his drinking, now, while he was down, adult-to-adult. I was shaky, maybe from the coffee I had snatched from the ICU visitor kitchen, or perhaps from feeling like the little girl about to challenge my daddy. As a family counselor, I knew all about addiction, though until now I had been too spineless to apply what I knew to my own family.

Dad pointed to his untouched dinner tray—applesauce, mashed potatoes, some sort of green soup. "You eat it," he told me.

I picked up his spoon and devoured the rejected hospital food, lukewarm and gross. Afterward, I ducked into his bathroom and threw water on my face. I looked in the mirror, saw the circles under my eyes, and convinced myself I was no longer his little girl. When I came back, he was almost asleep.

I began my intervention speech. "I love you."

He smiled. We rarely said this in our family.

"I hate your drinking."

He looked out the window.

"You get quiet. Angry. Mean."

He refused to look at me.

"We want you to stop." I didn't really know if I was speaking for the whole family, but it sounded better than speaking only for myself.

A slight nod as he stared out the window at the ventilation system on the roof. "Never enough," he said, hoarse-voiced.

He went on, his words barely audible.

"Never good enough."

"What do you mean?"

"At work. Not enough."

"What about those awards?"

He shook his head.

"Never enough when I was a kid. Dad gone, not enough to eat, too many kids."

"Not enough to go around," I said. Food, money, or affection. Growing up in the Depression, survival was the goal.

"I did my best with you kids. Don't you know that? Isn't that enough?"

Before I could answer, he began to snore. I stared at his empty tray, embarrassed, like I had just seen him naked, stripped of all that tough working man's gear. I thought of how alike we were, how I never felt like I was strong enough, smart enough, or accomplished enough. Always trying to reach a goal that led to another, bigger one.

I kissed his cheek and tiptoed out the door.

For three years after his first heart attack, Dad rallied and crashed several times. Initially, he attended cardio rehab, ate the recommended heart-healthy diet Mom cooked for him, stopped smoking, decreased his drinking and lost weight. The ER doctor who took him from the paramedics was wrong. Dad was alive and mostly healthy. But sometimes he relapsed, drank too much, binged on pastries, potato chips, and candy. Then he developed an allergy to mosquitoes resulting in severe swelling at the location of each bite. He tried taking allergy shots, but his reaction to each shot was worse than the bite, making the shots riskier than the mosquitoes. He took up smoking again, claiming it kept the mosquitoes away, and built himself a mosquito net so he could still sit out and enjoy the lake at the cabin. Then after a sobering visit to his cardiologist, he quit smoking and drinking again.

I slid out of my sleeping bag from where I'd slept on the floor of Mom's sewing room. My head throbbed, throat burned, lips like shriveled leaves. I needed aspirin and coffee. Decades of residue from both parents' cigarette smoking clung to their clothes, furniture, and walls, making it difficult for me to breathe. Though Dad had quit several times Mom continued to smoke. She was in the kitchen now smoking with my sister Patty.

I felt cheated. Just the week before I had stopped at my parents' duplex to visit, where Dad was assembling supplies to work on the cabin. He was sober, cheerful, and looking forward to a weekend of getting the greenhouse he had built ready for planting. He seemed once again to be the guy who could fix anything, maybe even his own failing body.

But now he was gone. I had planned to spend more time with him, to ask him to help me remember the landscape of the town where I grew up, and which had grown so quickly into a city. The place where we picked blueberries before the shopping mall obliterated the marsh. The creek—now drained for a housing development—where we sat on the bank and swatted mosquitoes while he fished. The topography of the land before it was transformed by the Great Earthquake. Maybe we could have been close again, like the days when we skated on Lake Spenard or worked together to wire his friend's new cabin. Now that chance was gone.

I last saw his body as the morticians wheeled him away, wrapped in thick black plastic, like an oversized suit bag with a zipper. The young assistant opened the bag far enough for me to see Dad's sallow face, lips slightly apart, eyes closed, long dark lashes resting against his cheek. I had rushed to the house from my job at the bank, pulled from a training session I was conducting. I had no time to process the news, too shocked and numb to grieve. His death was not unexpected, but still, at sixty-three, he seemed so young.

Mom pulled a chipped white mug from the kitchen cupboard, poured coffee from her ancient Mr. Coffee machine, and handed it to me. I added milk from a gallon jug, stirred slowly, and sipped the strong, bitter liquid. It was a stale, cheap brand from the back of the cupboard, but a few sips coupled with aspirin tamped down my headache. Patty and I were staying with Mom to help her get through the first days of what would become twenty years without my dad. (Our sister Teri had moved to California with her partner and would not arrive until Dad's funeral.) What struck me as I sat with my mother and sister and planned Dad's funeral was how he had abandoned me to a family of women with whom I had little in common. Neither my mother nor sisters shared my love of wild places, the outdoors, or travel. Dad was the storyteller, the history keeper, the risk-taker willing to leave a safe urban life for a place he had never seen, the one who inspired me to get outside, travel, and explore wild places.

In all her years of worrying about Dad's health, nagging him to eat better, lose weight, stop drinking, Mom never prepared for the inevitability of him dying before she did. Now her caretaking job was over. She would need money, but she was not sure how much she had or how much she required. She restarted her litany—*I should have known, I could have, if only*. She still couldn't drive, and her children and grandchildren had their own lives to live, but we would have to find a way to help her. I thought of losing Jim and wondered if I would be as unprepared and immobilized as Mom. How would I keep going?

I felt Dad's absence as missing pieces of my own life story. When I tried to remember the details of an event from my childhood, I could no longer call upon him to ask. Where was that mountain where he shot the Dall sheep? Who was the friend he asked to pick me up at Girl Scout camp in his floatplane? Did he ever change his mind about girls and college? Though his loss was an emptiness that never went away, it would be years before I would really grieve for him.

I was left with the one compliment from Dad I would carry with me. When he worked at the hospital, he took the risk of hiring a woman to be the groundskeeper—maintaining the trees, gardens, and interior plants at the hospital, and in winter operating all the equipment needed for snow removal—a job that was until then exclusively male. He marveled at her ability, he said, to work "just like a man." A woman, he made sure to say, who reminded him of me.

I returned to the cabin with Mom and Jim on Memorial Day, ten years after my first visit. The last shards of ice had finally dissolved on the lake. Mom asked me to row her across the water to Dad's favorite fishing spot. It was only the two of us. My sister Patty said she was not comfortable participating in what we were about to do, and Teri didn't have the money to fly back from California. I dreaded our task but felt it was my duty to help Mom, and to respect Dad's wishes.

Mom sat in the bow while I rowed. She held a colorful tin box containing Dad's ashes. It looked like it should hold cookies instead. The squawking of our human-propelled boat raked against the early morning quiet since neither of us had thought to oil the oarlocks on the old metal rowboat—that was Dad's job. With each dip the oars screeched in protest and a knot between my shoulders tightened.

When we reached a spot too deep for grass or lily pads to reach the surface, Mom told me to stop. Rays of sunlight streaked through the top few feet of the murky water. Mom placed the box between her knees, opened the lid, and drew out a thick plastic bag that appeared to contain chunks of broken white coral. As she untwisted the metal fastener, I realized I had not prepared anything to say. I should have found a poem, pulled something from the Bible, written a few words. Now nothing profound came to mind. I thought Mom would say some last words to Dad. Maybe she spoke to him silently, but we sat together without speaking for a few minutes.

Mom dipped her hand into the bag, pulled out a handful of ashes, and scattered the bits into the water. They dropped like oddly shaped pebbles. When she'd tossed out half the contents, she handed the bag to me. I couldn't bring myself to touch the bleached-out remnants of my dad's body, so I tipped the bag and sprinkled the rest of the pieces into the water. Most of them slowly floated away, some larger pieces sunk quickly out of sight.

"Back to the fish, Dad," is all I said.

Neither one of us cried. I passed the bag back to Mom. She stuffed it into the tin, wiggled the lid back on, and tucked it under her seat. I pictured the ashes sliding toward the bottom, fish poised to intercept them on the way down.

Nearby, a grebe laughed, then dived. A slight breeze gently rocked the boat. I felt the expanse of the lake, its coves and false horizons, its peninsulas and boggy fingers, the creeks and trickles running in and out of it. The peace and beauty that lured Dad here made a rare appearance. I breathed deeply and my shoulders relaxed.

The cabin belonged to Mom now, but since she didn't drive, one of us had to drive seventy-five miles to get her there. My sisters still felt a sentimental attachment to the place, particularly Teri, who had returned to Alaska a year after Mom and I scattered Dad's ashes and was now living here with her partner Wally. Teri had spent her teenage years at the cabin hanging out with friends, running dad's boat, racing his snow mobile across the frozen lake. When Elisha entered her teenage years, she enjoyed the same fast toys that endeared Teri to the place. Often on those busy weekends when we visited the cabin I felt hemmed in, overwhelmed by speed and noise, and sad at how this peaceful lake had been overcome by thrill seekers. Simple weekend cabins were being squeezed out by retirement homes and second residences.

Years passed. Elisha graduated from high school, attended college outside of Alaska for two years, then returned to complete her business degree at the University of Alaska. Before she completed college, and using money left to her by her paternal grandfather, she purchased her first condo, then quickly her second one, and married her high school boyfriend. Unlike me, she had no need to rush into marriage just to escape her mother's life. Nor did she have any reservations about having children. Within two years she and her husband Chad had two children, Cason and Carly, just nineteen months apart. In the meantime, my career path shifted more than once, from counseling, to corporate training and consulting, to public school administration, and to a doctorate degree in human and organizational development. I was always learning, searching, striving to have more and more effective tools to make the world a better place, but really trying to achieve an ever-elusive sense of competence and confidence in whatever work I did.

For the next several years after Dad's death, the cabin lay empty for much of the time, and with no regular maintenance it began to deteriorate. First the mice, which we attacked with poison, then the carpenter ants found the cabin's rotting wood irresistible. Efficient and industrious, the fat black bugs were turning the whole structure into a sawdust pile. Worse, as the cabin strained with the seasonal undulations of the marsh beneath, it was splitting apart at its fault line. The two halves withdrew from each other as if they could no longer endure an intimacy they'd never truly accepted.

Mom nagged us to do *something* to save the disintegrating place. Teri's husband Wally, a building contractor, gave the cabin a thorough check-up and declared it terminal, roof splitting apart, walls hollowed out by ant excavation, foundation disintegrating into the swamp. Dad wanted the cabin to stay in the family, a place his grandkids and great grandkids could enjoy long after he was gone. We gathered one Saturday—Mom, daughters, husbands, and adult grandchildren—and agreed the best option forward, short of selling the place, was to tear down the old structure and build a new one. In memory of Dad. For Mom. For our kids.

Wally drew up a simple plan for the new cabin. We would demolish the old cabin and build the new one ourselves, using a portion of the small estate Dad left Mom to purchase materials with Wally's contractor's discounts.

One weekend in May we convened at the old cabin—Mom, Jim and me; Teri and Wally with their son Bryan; Patty and her son Jim; Elisha, husband Chad, and elementary-aged children Cason and Carly. We arrived in pickup trucks, carrying sledgehammers, saws, and crowbars for our assault on the rotten wooden structure. We ripped out nails, tore down walls, loaded debris into the trucks for the dump, and built a colossal bonfire by the lake to burn most of the scraps. We set up a table using additional scraps of plywood and sawhorses, spread out a plastic tablecloth from inside the cabin, and laid out sandwiches, chips, beer, soda, cookies and pie. Never before had we worked so closely as a family. Mom stood on the sidelines, agitated we had taken over her cabin, yelling at us to be careful, worrying someone would get hurt. We reminded her again and again that this was what she wanted, what she agreed to, but she could not let go of wanting to control how we carried out the work. We salvaged the wood stove, refrigerator, propane cookstove, and most of the keepsakes that had adorned the interior walls.

Over the next few weekends family members rotated in and out, hauling in lumber for the new cabin, hauling out trash from the old, until only a gravel pad and tool shed were left of Mom's and Dad's retirement dream. I felt a strange peace at clearing away the dilapidated cabin and starting over. Now we could build it right.

As with any strictly volunteer project, commitment and energy sometimes stalled. Wally led the reconstruction, with Jim adding expertise from having built a cabin with his father as a teenager. We followed their lead, completing the foundation (posts on concrete pads), the framing, and the walls. Wally got called to paying projects, so could not finish the rest of the cabin before winter. Not wanting to let all our work deteriorate in the snow and cold weather, Mom used more of her money to hire a contractor and roof the structure. Over the next spring and early summer Jim, and I, Chad and Elisha, and Teri and Wally worked on insulating the cabin and finishing the interior.

We finally completed the project in late summer the year after we started. We hung pictures from the old cabin inside the new one—Dad smiling in his captain's hat, one of Jim's pictures of a ptarmigan changing from its winter white plumage to summer buff and brown. We filled the new cabin with furniture cast out of our homes. My sister Teri sewed cheery blue and green curtains and hung them over the new windows. Now the place we'd built looked clean, bright, and cozy. I stood back one morning, amazed at what we'd accomplished together, with our own hands. Dad would have been proud of his daughters, his family, and the stout construction of the new cabin. Mom could relax knowing the job was complete, and no one was injured in the process.

Chapter Ten

In her twenty years of widowhood, Mom had lived long enough to watch her children and grandchildren grow to adulthood, and to enjoy her six great-grandchildren. She rented a two-bedroom duplex apartment in a quiet neighborhood bordering on one of the last remaining parcels of undeveloped former homestead land in the city. Her large living room window looked out on a dense spruce forest that must have reminded her of our house near Lake Spenard so long ago. The place had a small kitchen with an adjoining dining area. She furnished it with some of the furniture left from the house she and Dad had owned when Elisha was still in preschool—a green sofa, a bright red and brown striped chair, Dad's big gray recliner.

My office at the University of Alaska was about ten minutes from where she lived. Earning my doctorate allowed me the opportunity to obtain a job with the School of Social Work under a grant to conduct child welfare research and program evaluation.

At eighty-two years old, Mom was in the early phases of emphysema. Though she had quit smoking three years before, her lungs were already quite damaged. She had other health problems she didn't share, however, which we didn't know about. She began to refuse our invitations to lunch or family gatherings, her own birthday party, and to church with her friend Grace, who at eighty-seven years old still drove. Mom's excuses did not make sense. "I ate something bad." Or, "It's too cold outside." Or, "It's too much trouble." She loved spending time with her grandkids and great-grandkids, so I didn't know what was wrong with her.

Fine, I told myself. I wouldn't invite her again.

In truth, it was easier not to pay attention, easier to leave Mom at her apartment. Easier not to have to drive all the way from our house in south Anchorage near the mountains to the northeast side of town to pick her up, take her out, then drive all the way back to her apartment and home again.

Eventually, we three sisters began to compare notes regarding our visits to Mom. The food one of us would drop off on Monday would still sit uneaten on her refrigerator shelf on Thursday. Whenever we called, she took a long time to answer and would be wheezing when she talked. When Teri stopped by one day, she noticed Mom had quit doing any laundry.

The three of us coordinated our schedules to jointly escort Mom to her medical appointments and find out what was going on—three daughters and an old lady crowding into a tiny examining room. What followed was a cascade of doctors, appointments, and diagnoses. A valve in her heart was leaking (probably damaged by years of smoking) and a chest X-ray revealed spots on her lungs. She was put on blood thinners and referred to a pulmonologist who advised her she needed surgery to biopsy the spots. While we were trying to weigh the risks of proceeding with lung surgery, she suffered a bowel obstruction and had to have emergency abdominal surgery, which revealed she had colon cancer. She had never had a colonoscopy despite having assured us repeatedly that, yes, she would get one as soon as she could get an appointment. A follow-up PET scan revealed the colon cancer had spread to her liver and lungs. At some point, because of her abdominal surgery, she was taken off blood thinners, and quickly developed blood clots in both legs—which required another emergency surgery. During Mom's second hospital stay, we met with the palliative care physician who revealed that Mom was not going to get better, and explained what we could expect over the next few months as her body quit functioning. She could return home, the doctor told us, but would require twenty-four-hour care. Teri volunteered to take Mom in, but we all knew it was unrealistic. She had a full-time job and there was no room in her house for another person. Neither Patty nor I felt willing or capable of shouldering that kind of responsibility. Instead, we contacted a licensed home care agency.

On a dark January morning Patty, Teri, and I waited in Mom's apartment for the third caregiver the agency had sent. When Patty answered the door Eva walked in. "Hi honey," she said, and dropped a duffel bag we later found out contained her thrift-store clothes, romance novels, and a Bible.

Honey? In our family we reserved that kind of coziness for babies and toddlers.

By the time the agency sent Eva to Mom's doorstep, she had already fired two other caregivers. Or had they fired her? We never got the full story from the elder care agency, but Mom, revealing a prejudice and sense of privilege she rarely exhibited, made some remarks that could have been clues.

"She's Eskimo, you know." (Explaining why the woman was late to her shift.)

Or, "That little Oriental lady, I can't understand a word she says." (Explaining why Mom didn't talk to her.)

Mom couldn't even remember their names.

Eva slipped out of her boots and swept off her wool hat, her wispy blond hair electrified around her plump face. She caught us off guard when she hugged each of us to her ample chest, then planted a smooch on Mom's cheek.

In her recliner beside the oxygen tank, Mom winced and blushed.

"We're going to have a good time together," Eva said.

I exchanged glances with Patty and Teri, the youngest sister. Who was this woman and what did she want?

Eva grabbed a chair from the kitchen table and scooted it right next to Mom.

"Now, what do you like to eat?" she asked with an accent that sounded faintly German, or maybe Scandinavian. She moved her face close to Mom's. Maybe she thought Mom was hard of hearing. "I fix whatever you like, dear." She patted Mom's bony hand with her short, thick fingers.

Mom looked away, at the reflection of the two of them shining in the living room window. "I don't know what the fuss is about," Mom said. "I was doing fine on my own. I don't need anybody."

Mom was *not* doing fine. Neither were we. We were exhausted from driving back and forth to the emergency room on dark, icy nights, scanning the roads for wandering moose. From taking shifts spending nights and days watching over Mom in her tiny apartment. From trying to get her to take her medicine and eat *something*. All this togetherness while juggling jobs, husbands, children, and grandchildren wore us down. I had already compressed my workweek at the university in order to watch my grandkids one day a week. And we sisters were not so close that we chitchatted on the phone, went shopping together, or watched each other's kids. We usually picked up the family news from the gossip Mom spread liberally among us.

Mom took to Eva right away. Cook, housekeeper, nurse, storyteller—but most of all, listener—Eva pampered Mom like she was a celebrity. She prepared whatever concoctions Mom said she liked to eat, sending one of us to the store with her list of groceries, paying no attention to whether they were healthy or not. After a few days, Mom seemed more alert and energetic. Maybe all the socializing helped.

Knowing Mom's time was running out, family members rotated in and out of her apartment, Eva welcoming everyone. Elisha brought Cason and Carly; Patty's daughter Jackie arrived with her daughters Katie and baby Grace; Patty's son Jim with his wife and twins; then Teri, Wally, and Bryan; and on weekends my Jim came with me. It didn't take Eva long to sort out which children, grandchildren, and husbands belonged with which of us daughters, a daunting task. She got everyone's names right, too, a task Mom frequently fumbled.

A week after Eva made her entrance, I stopped by to deliver the items from her shopping list—ice cream, fudge sauce, steak, insulin needles, and a porta-potty—and found her and Mom sitting in the living room giggling. From the expressions on their faces when I came in, I had the feeling they'd been talking about me.

I put the bags on the kitchen table. "What's so funny?" I asked.

"Your mom was just telling me about how your daughter got suspended from high school for fighting." Eva snorted. "It's hilarious. That beautiful little blond daughter of yours. Fighting. Over a boy. Right there in the hall."

Eva only knew Elisha as a well-dressed business professional woman working in commercial real estate, not the wild teenager with a continual string of suitors tapping at her bedroom window. Mom chuckled. "You made her stay with your dad and me as punishment. Remember? Sister Arlene came by and told us the other girl came from a bad family and was a real troublemaker. You were trying to be so strict. We had a great time with her while you were working."

I groaned. This was not my favorite family story, especially since I worked for the school administration back then and knew the principal who suspended my daughter. But with twenty years distance I had to admit there was some humor in the incident. I marveled at the relaxed and indulgent woman my mother was as a grandmother. Patient, playful, curious, and most of all with none of the angry predictions of failure she had heaped on me.

One day Eva somehow managed to extract Mom from the house and drive her to lunch. This meant carrying Mom's oxygen tank while maneuvering her out the door, down the sidewalk, into the car, into the restaurant, and finally repeating the whole process in reverse. We're not sure how she accomplished this miracle, but Mom praised the trip like it was some exotic adventure. Eva also eased the burden of transporting Mom to her legion of medical specialists. She would pack Mom's wheelchair in the back of her Subaru, then load Mom in the front seat. One or more of us would meet them at the doctor's office, help unload the wheelchair, and wheel Mom into the building while Eva parked the car, then joined us to supply the doctor with new details about Mom's ailments.

It was hard not to fall in love with Eva—the easy way she greeted me with "Hi, honey" and those chest-crushing hugs. I envied the way she was so open with her affection and the way Mom embraced her so easily and thrived in her company. I felt so guarded around Mom, so defended against her neediness, so ready for her rejection. Before Eva, I'd walk into Mom's apartment and feel like a fifty-pound weight had dropped on my chest. It was more than the accumulated layers of cigarette smoke in her apartment and on her clothes. Mom saw no need for education, travel, or current events. To prove to myself how different I was, I collected degrees like trophies and grabbed every chance I could to pursue some far-off adventure, all in an effort to be smarter, more successful, and more courageous than Mom. She wasn't interested in my work, travels, or friends. We had little to talk about except her grandchildren and great-grandchildren. I felt guilty I didn't want to spend time with her, nor was I willing to sacrifice the quality of my life at home with Jim to take her in.

Beyond her expertise at managing Mom's care, Eva coordinated her own family's lives from a distance. Rather than commute forty miles each way every day on a dark highway prone to moose crossings, Eva slept in Mom's spare bedroom and worked her week straight through, close by in case Mom needed any help at night. By day, Eva stayed connected with her large extended family by cell phone. During my visits, I'd catch fragments of her conversations: Advice to her daughter on the new baby's rash. An invitation to Sunday dinner for her granddaughter. A reminder to her husband to schedule maintenance on the Subaru. Long, indecipherable chats with her own mother in what we now knew was their native Croatian. I could barely manage work, husband, time with my grandkids, and Mom's doctor's appointments.

Whenever I stopped by Mom's apartment, Eva asked about my work, my daughter, my grandkids. She told stories about the old people she had cared for, about the children she'd raised, on and on. It was easy to linger.

One day when a quick lunchtime dash from work ended with me staying longer than I should have over coffee and sticky buns, Eva made a surprising pronouncement.

"Your mom was a real pioneer," she said.

Mom beamed and nodded. "I've been telling Eva about when we first came to Alaska."

"So brave," Eva said, "leaving her whole family to come to Alaska with your dad."

Brave? I never thought of Mom that way. She depended too much on other people. Besides, she had the support of Dad's family for that first year, until the car accident that killed his parents. But I remembered our last day in Buffalo as we waited at the train station, dressed up as if we were on our way to church though we were leaving our home for good, and no one knew when they would see each other again.

Mom continued telling her story to Eva.

"My mother tried to convince me to stay in Buffalo until Paul found work and got settled," Mom said. "But no, my place was with my husband, so I went."

"I bet it was real tough," Eva said.

"Paul didn't have a job when we got here," Mom continued, "and we didn't even have a car."

Another memory coasted back from our time living in the rabbit hutches in Spenard. A snowstorm. We needed groceries. Dad bundled up for the long trek along the highway to the grocery store. Mom told me she was worried he would get run over or freeze to death. In Buffalo, we rode buses everywhere we wanted to go, but you did not venture out on foot in a snowstorm. In my child's mind, Dad was the brave one.

"You must have been so lonely, Dorothy."

I'd always taken our "coming to Alaska" family story for granted; most people I knew had such stories of their migrations north. But now, through Eva's eyes, I glimpsed the risks Mom took and how hard life must have been in her wild new home. Without her family, without the familiar surroundings of the town where she was born, without the ability to go from place to place, Mom must have felt utterly alone. But what choice did she have? At that time a woman's role was to get married, have children, and support her husband in his choices, hoping those choices would provide enough money to care for everyone. Once, when Patty and I were young and our parents had just bought our small house in Spenard, Mom took a job as a typist on the military base, riding to work with Dad every day. The only childcare option then was to find a stay-at-home mom to watch us. First, we stayed with the wife of one of Dad's co-workers who lived in a trailer with no bathroom. After I got locked in the trailer park's public restroom and experienced the panic of not being able to get out until someone came to rescue me, we moved to daycare in another home of someone Dad knew. The wife was kind, but her husband was abusive to her and their two boys. He would make his wife call him in sick at his railroad job, then watch TV all day, slapping his kids around for any small infraction. So Mom gave up working after just a few months. It was simply too stressful and costly to leave us with someone else. That was the last time she had any means of earning her own money.

As I thought about Mom's situation, I admitted my marriage to Ron at such a young age was in part to have the financial means to get through college and have more choices in life than Mom. It would have taken me several more years, probably working more than one job at a time, simply to earn my undergraduate degree. When I divorced Ron at age thirty, I discovered as a single woman I did not exist in the eyes of most financial institutions. I had no credit history and could not even buy my first car without the generosity of a newly formed women's credit union. Later, without Jim's help and my student loans, I never would have been able to earn my doctorate and gain any sort of financial independence. Being completely honest with myself, I realized without my partnership with Jim I would be considerably less prosperous.

As I finished my coffee and wiped the sugary residue from my mouth, Eva resumed the story she'd begun before I arrived. She had followed her husband to a faraway land, leaving Croatia before the Bosnian War erupted and settling in Ohio where he found work. Things quickly went wrong in their new country. When Eva's husband began to abuse her physically and mentally, she scooped up her twin baby girls and left him. With limited English, she worked two and three jobs to support herself and her daughters—tending bar, waiting tables, cleaning houses, whatever she could find. She relied on friends to help care for the girls. During those years, she said, sleep was a luxury she could seldom afford.

While tending bar, she met a man who was kind to her and the girls. The two became friends and eventually married. From Ohio, she migrated even farther from her home, to Barrow (renamed Utqiagvik), Alaska, an Inupiat town of 4,000 located on the northernmost tip of the United States. Surprisingly diverse, with immigrants from China, Korea, Thailand, the Philippines, Mexico, and many other countries, the community welcomed Eva and her willingness to work hard as a teacher's aide. She and her new husband had two more children, and when they moved closer to Anchorage for his job, she became a home health caregiver.

As I reflected on the stories of the three of us in the room, I recognized each of us had chosen, in our own ways, to make sacrifices that would create better lives for ourselves and our children.

Chapter Eleven

A few days later I stopped for another lunchtime visit. As I let myself in, I overheard Eva singing at the back of the apartment. Her voice was strong and clear and as I caught the words, I realized she was singing a hymn, something about angels and heaven.

No one sang in our family—except in church—and I hadn't been to church since my niece Jackie's marriage several years back. Unable to commit to a set of beliefs offered by any one faith, I dropped out of organized religion shortly after I married Ron. My sisters also gave up their connection to the Catholic Church, or any church for that matter, and I hadn't raised my daughter in any kind of spiritual tradition.

I followed Eva's voice down the hallway to Mom's bedroom and stood at the doorway.

"Hi, honey." Bent over Mom's bed, Eva glanced up. "Mom doesn't want to get up today."

"Too tired," Mom mumbled.

Eva hummed while gently washing Mom's face, patting it with a towel, then brushing her thin white hair. Around them were angels. On the dresser. Hanging from the doorknob. Perched on top of the lamp. Lacy, white plastic angels, the kind you would see decorating one of those *Give to a child in need* Christmas trees in a mall, each a slight variation on the next. My growing acceptance of Eva's warm ways shifted to annoyance that she would spread her religious paraphernalia around Mom's house. I didn't believe in angels, plastic or otherwise.

Had Eva asked Mom's permission to adorn the room? I had no idea what exchanges went on between them when I wasn't around. Not that Mom would have argued. She believed in angels, saints, miracles, lighting candles to carry your prayers to God.

"Oops," Eva said as she helped Mom shift positions. "We're going to need to change your bedclothes, sweetie."

While Eva went to the closet for clean linens, I helped Mom up to use the porta-potty beside the bed. I fumbled for a firm grip on her arms, loose flesh slipping through my hands like half-melted gelatin. Her skin was as warm and soft as a baby's, but I hated touching it, touching her. She was dissolving, the extra fat she'd carried for so many years evaporating from her body, leaving nothing but loose curtains of skin. As I pulled her up, she grasped my arm. Old IV bruises spread like spilled coffee across the knotted veins crisscrossing her once delicate hands. In these hands I could see my future, the inevitable failing of my own body.

I left the room while Eva bathed Mom and changed her clothes and sheets. When Eva finished, I followed her into the laundry room to help. At least I could do that much. As we stuffed the soiled sheets into the washing machine, Eva whispered, "Not long now, honey. The angels will come for her soon."

I wanted to ask her how she knew, and why she was telling me, and what I was supposed to do with that knowledge. Instead, I said nothing as I poured laundry detergent over the clothes. Eva had witnessed more than one old person pass from this life to whatever came next, and I trusted she knew the signs life was running out. I didn't want to talk about any of that now, didn't know *how* to talk about it.

A few days later, while I was at work, Eva coaxed Mom out of bed, sat her in the living room recliner, and brought her a piece of buttered toast and a cup of weak tea with plenty of sugar the way Mom liked it. As Mom slowly crunched on her toast, Eva told me later, they chatted while Mom looked out at the old spruce tree in the front yard. Eva noticed Mom had quit chewing and simply stared out the window. Eva rushed to the recliner and leaned into Mom's face.

"Dorothy," Eva said. "Wake up."

Mom grunted.

Eva pushed the "lifeline" button Mom wore on a cord around her neck to summon the paramedics. Then she called my sister Patty.

"Come quick!" she told Patty. "I think your mom's having a stroke!"

Patty called me at work. "The paramedics are taking Mom to the emergency room," she said. "Eva's with her. I'll meet you there."

As I gathered up my coat and shut down my computer, I wondered why Eva had called Patty, not me, the oldest sister. Maybe Eva felt closer to Patty, or maybe she didn't think

I'd know what to do, or maybe she assumed I wouldn't care enough to get there on time. In some irrational way, I thought I had failed Eva and Mom.

I circled the hospital parking lot several times before I found a space. By the time I reached the door to the ER, my hands were trembling—from my dash from work, the traffic, my morning coffee, from dread at what I was about to face. I gave the security guard Mom's name and he buzzed open the ER door. A plump, middle-aged woman rushed over to meet me. A brass nameplate on her sweater read *Chaplain*.

"You must be the third daughter," she said. "I'll take you to your mom."

The last one to arrive.

In all of Mom's ER crises—the heart problems, the obstructed bowel, the blood clots in her legs—I'd never had a chaplain's escort before. She led me to a small room with a big glass sliding door. Teri, Patty, and Eva, still in their coats, huddled around Mom, nodded, and squeezed together to make room for me. Head slightly elevated, Mom lay on a small gurney, mostly hidden under layers of white blankets. Wires stretched from various parts of her body to blinking and beeping machines.

"Hi Mom."

Her eyes moved my way, but she said nothing.

I recalled Eva's premonition in the laundry room and the procession of angels in the bedroom. If Mom was dying, she'd want a priest, someone to perform the last rites to help her get ready for whatever came next. I don't know why I felt so strongly about this since I had given up the Catholic faith long ago, but I knew it would be important for Mom, and the presence of a priest would bring her comfort. At my request, the chaplain left to summon one.

Patty, Teri, Eva, and I usurped most of the space in Mom's tiny room, ignoring the One Guest Only sign. Nurses and technicians came and went, came and went. *Tests*, they said. *We're running tests*. We waited. And waited. Stealing chairs from other rooms. Throwing our coats and purses on them. Bumping into each other and all the gear in the room.

Mom's mind evaporated in front of us. Each time the hospital staff posed a question, a piece of her floated away. First, she forgot her birth date, then forgot the names of those of us in the room, then lost her ability to separate one word from the next. Words tumbled from her mouth all together, indecipherable.

I tried to help. Thinking she was thirsty, I filled a paper cup with water, stuck a straw in it, and held it for her. When she tried to drink, she choked. *Oh, no*, I thought, *she's aspirated the water*. But after a few gasps, she started breathing again.

Two hours passed, then three. I'd had enough waiting. While Eva and my sisters encircled Mom, I ducked out of the room and grabbed a passing doctor.

"Isn't my mom supposed to have that drug?" I asked, pointing to the room I just left. "The one that stops the damage from a stroke?" I had read about it in some journal.

He paused, maybe trying to figure out who I was and what I was talking about. He glanced into Mom's room. "Too risky for an elderly person with as many health problems as your mom," he told me, and sprinted away. What could be riskier than forgetting how to swallow?

A short time later, they moved Mom from the ER to a hospital ward. To die, though none of us said it.

Twenty years earlier, my dad had retired as the maintenance manager of this same hospital, and even then the wing where they moved my mom was called "the place of no return." That much hadn't changed. None of the patients there were ambulatory. I don't think anyone ever left on their own two feet. They either exited with a sheet over their heads, or on a gurney into a waiting transport ambulance for the final trip home, or to a nursing home. At least Mom's room was private and quiet, nothing like the cramped glass room where she had first been parked, with the constant buzz and ding of machines and staff zipping from one patient to the next. Most of the rooms in this wing now appeared to be storage areas with discarded or broken hospital equipment, and all of the other patients in the wing were so far away there was not much traffic near Mom's room.

Eva refused to leave Mom's bedside. I don't know whether it was her devotion to Mom, or if she didn't trust the hospital staff to take adequate care of her, or if she simply felt it was what she was paid to do. While my sisters and I rotated in and out of the hospital over the next two days, Eva stayed. On the second day Eva tried to get Mom to eat some of the pureed mush that had been delivered for lunch. Mom refused to open her mouth. Finally, Eva scooped up a spoonful of chocolate pudding from a bowl at the corner of the tray. When she held it under Mom's nose, Mom opened her lips and Eva deposited the sweet, dark substance on her tongue.

Mom smiled. "Tastes good," she said.

"Hooray!" Eva and I applauded. Mom was still there. She was coming back to us after all.

Those were the last words Mom would speak.

By the next day Eva had deep circles under her eyes, and

her clothes were stained and crumpled.

"Go home to your family," I told her.

She didn't want to leave, but it was our turn to take over. Teri, Patty, and I would work in shifts, I assured her. We wouldn't leave Mom alone. When at last I convinced her there was nothing for her to do until we could set up hospice care and take Mom home, she said she would leave as soon as Teri arrived for the first shift.

When I came back that night to relieve Teri, the same kind of plastic angels Eva had placed in Mom's bedroom now graced the windowsill of Mom's hospital room, buffers against the cold black night outside the window. "Eva?" I asked Teri as she left. She nodded. I decided I didn't mind their company. Mom was asleep, or at least her eyes were closed, so I unloaded my supplies for the night—coffee, energy bars, journal, book—then scooted a soft chair from the hallway into the room and placed it between Mom and the angels. I took hold of Mom's bony hand. Her skin was cool and soft, but translucent, like sheer rice paper covering her veins and tendons.

She moaned and clutched my hand. Her breathing stopped. Twenty seconds. Thirty. Forty. *Don't die, Mom.* She wheezed, a deep, rattling, greedy sucking of air, and grabbed the side rail. She kicked and tore off her sheets. Again, her breathing stopped. *Wait. Wait until Eva's here, or one of your other daughters. I can't do this alone.*

"It's okay to let go," I whispered. I followed the lie with an act of cowardice, running to find the night nurse. He returned with a liquid which he dropped onto Mom's tongue. For an hour or so, she was quiet. So began a long night. I wanted to believe in Eva's angels. I wanted to wipe away years of doubt, to know there was some reward for Mom's excruciating struggle to let go. But none of that thinking felt right.

The next day was Mom's eighty-third birthday. We sent out word that anyone who wanted to see Mom should come to the hospital. Mom's daughters and families arrived. Patty with her son Jim and his twins Damen and Aaron, and her daughter Jackie, she with children Katie and Grace; Teri, Bryan and Wally; Jim and I; Elisha and Chad with Cason and Carly. Someone brought paper, tape, balloons, markers, and cards. The kids scattered around the room and corridor with the art materials and made decorations, taping bright red, green, and blue hand-lettered *Happy Birthday, Grandma* posters to the walls. Someone streamed big-band music. The hospital staff even delivered a small freezer-burned birthday cake. Jackie held four-month-old Grace in her arms, the newest member of the family. People circulated around Mom's bed, whispering to her, touching her hands, kissing her cheeks. Had she been aware of it, she would have loved all the attention. Instead, she lay on her pillow, cheeks sunken, hair matted, lips cracked. The only sounds she uttered were grunts and gasps. Once, she grew agitated, tugging at her nightgown the way she'd torn at the covers the night before. My sisters and I quickly cleared the room of children and covered her. I was embarrassed for Mom. This is not what she would have wanted.

Just when I believed Mom's link to the outside world was completely severed, my daughter bent down to kiss her grandma on the forehead. As Elisha's long blond hair fell over her face, Mom opened her eyes, grabbed my daughter's silver necklace, pulled herself up, and mumbled an angry torrent of garbled syllables, as if to say, *Get me out of here*, or *I've had enough*. Startled, Elisha grabbed Mom's hand, then with her other hand disentangled Mom's fingers from the chain. Elisha drew back and rubbed the spot on her neck where the chain had chafed her skin. Mom dropped back onto her pillow with a long, rattling breath. Some shred of her was still inside, trying to break free.

In the morning, Patty, Teri, and I met at Mom's apartment, washed dishes, threw away food that had been sitting on the counter, took out the trash, and changed out the towels and sheets. We waited. Eva had returned to the hospital to accompany Mom in the transport van that would take her home. The hospice doctor arrived and, once the EMTs settled Mom in her own bed, he examined her. She was in the final stage of dying, he said. It was time to say goodbye.

I was relieved. I wanted it to be over. For Mom, with her shuddering breaths and her clenched fists, and selfishly, also for me. To imagine being trapped in a body that was shutting down bit by bit made my heart race. I was just four years shy of my dad's age when he died; I could be lying there sometime soon. I longed to escape Mom's dying, to come back when it was over.

All afternoon, many of the same family members who had come to the hospital rotated through her apartment, bringing food and stories, whispering in her ears, kissing her cheeks, saying goodbye. My nephew Jim's ex-wife Jill stopped to say goodbye. I did not know Mom had been especially supportive of her when she and Jim lost a baby a few years ago. Grace, the woman who befriended Mom in her early days in Alaska and frequently took her to Mass and breakfast on Sundays, also visited, weeping for the loss of one of her few remaining friends.

By evening, only Eva, Mom's daughters, and the angels

remained. Whether these were the same angels that had lined the hospital windowsill or a new collection—Eva, apparently, had an unending supply—they seemed to have as much right to the bedroom as we did, no less a part of the space than the glow-in-the dark crucifix that hung over the bed or the pictures of the grandkids scattered over the dingy lace cover on the dresser.

Mom's breaths were ragged and raspy, interspersed with long silences—we'd touch her neck to check for a pulse—followed by violent gulps of air. Still she kept fighting. We decided to give her the drugs the hospice doctor had left with us. Since she could no longer swallow, the drugs needed to go on her tongue, drop by drop. I couldn't see how we would ever get the liquid into her mouth and down her throat without choking her. Eva showed us what to do. She took the dropper, slid it into Mom's slightly opened lips, squeezed it, then held her lips closed. The liquid gurgled around for several minutes before slipping down her throat.

After a few minutes, Mom relaxed and breathed more easily, and as she relaxed, I relaxed. When the drugs wore off and Mom grew agitated again, we took turns squeezing doses into her mouth. I felt guilty drugging her, but she seemed so peaceful when she rested. Together, it seemed like we were doing the right thing. Helping each other help our mother. Eva was one of us, like a sister, like a mother, the kind of mother I wished I could be.

Devouring the comfort food people had brought, cinnamon rolls, poppy seed muffins, croissants, various cakes, all washed down with too much tea and coffee, we began to get giddy.

"All my girls have boobs big like me," Eva announced suddenly. "See how they'll turn out." She pointed to her breasts resting on her waistline.

"No worry about that in our family," said Patty. "We've all got Mom's tiny boobs."

"Except me," Teri joined in. "When you put on an extra thirty pounds, some of it goes to your boobs."

We giggled, then guffawed. It felt like a middle school slumber party. A great relief swept through my body, along with something I hadn't felt in weeks: joy. We laughed about how little our mothers taught us about sex and our periods, and how we over-corrected by swamping our kids with more sex ed than they wanted to know.

"Wait," I said, spent from releasing so much laughter. "Mom can hear us. Should we be talking about this stuff now?"

"Honey," said Eva. "Your mom is blessed to have her daughters here with her. She'd be laughing, too, if she could."

A few hours later, I awoke next to Patty on Mom's lumpy pull-out sofa. My throat was dry. I needed water. The place smelled like cigarettes from my sister's clothes and hair, sweat from all of us, and garbage needing emptying. I shuffled to the kitchen, found a clean glass, and filled it with water. Dirty dishes and silverware filled the sink and the empty packages from baked goods covered the counter and table. I needed air. A shower. Space.

Back in Mom's bedroom, Eva and Teri sat on either side of Mom's bed, each holding a hand, each stroking her face. Eva looked up and smiled.

"She's still here, honey."

Mom's breaths were faint. I watched Eva and my youngest sister for a few minutes. Tender and serene. Eva's soothing words: "We're here, Dorothy. It's okay to go. We love you."

I wanted to be more like them. Patient. Giving. Calm. But I needed out. I needed life. Movement. Breath.

"I need a break," I said. "I'll be back soon."

I put on my boots and coat and got in my car. As I drove home in the dark, snow crystals shimmered in my headlights. More than anything, I wanted to ski, to gulp the icy air and feel myself slicing through the fresh snow, to glide until I was worn out, the kind of exhaustion that comes from arms, legs, heart, a whole body working the way it was meant to. But when I got home I crawled into bed, next to my husband. He wrapped his body around mine, slow even breaths against my skin, lips on my neck. I lay there, savoring the pleasure of our bodies and lives together. Had Mom been happy in her life? Her safe, simple life in Alaska, the one she had bequeathed to all of us?

I slid out of bed, took a steaming shower, and headed back to Mom's apartment. When I crept into the bedroom, Teri was standing beside the bed. Eva was holding Mom's hand. It was purple.

Eva looked up. "Teri and I were chatting and we looked over and waited for her next breath, but it never came," she said.

I wasn't there. I should have waited. I was too selfish, thinking of my own needs. But Patty left right after I did. And Teri was there. And Eva. Maybe it was easier for Mom, to go without her older daughters hovering, worrying.

No longer struggling, Mom lay in her bed, looking as soft

and peaceful as a sleeping baby. I kissed her cold cheek. Teri and Eva would wash Mom's body before the mortician came. I couldn't bring myself to join in this final intimacy. Throughout her whole life, I had never seen her naked.

I left the room. Patty arrived and waited with me in the living room while Teri and Eva dressed Mom in a soft new cotton nightgown, tucked the covers around her body, and positioned her head on a pillow.

The hospice chaplain arrived. We joined hands around Mom's bed. In the presence of Eva's angels he led us in the Lord's Prayer. At first I was rusty with the words, but as our voices mingled and we repeated the verses, I took comfort in the familiar ritual. Maybe something sacred was taking place. Together we were honoring Mom and each other.

Eva and Teri cried loud, bountiful tears. Patty sniffled and wiped her eyes. I remained dry-eyed. To Eva, perhaps, I'd succumbed to the comfort of the angels. In truth, I was sad but relieved, grateful Mom's suffering was over.

After the morticians collected Mom's body, I returned to the bedroom, though no one had need of me there. The white plastic angels were gone. Eva must have packed them into her duffel bag, ready for her next assignment, for the next family, flawed and yet filled with love.

The summer after Mom died, after her ashes were mingled with Dad's in Nancy Lake, I deeded my share of the cabin to Elisha, knowing she would help my sisters take good care of it. I could finally let go.

Part Two

Chapter Twelve

My bike sang its own symphony down the path to Little Campbell Creek. Seat springs creaking, frame rattling like my bones, stones zinging off the spokes, fat tires crunching in loose gravel. Wind whistled through my purple helmet. No one was on the trail. No one waited for me and no one knew I was there. I was free. And I had to make up for lost time.

Thigh-high grass waved and glistened as the sun peeked in and out of the birch forest. I glanced side-to-side for dark objects lurking between the trees. Though I was less than half a mile from my house, this was bear country and I had forgotten my bear spray. So I whistled loudly to my imaginary dog Dirk, the Doberman, who I pretended was racing beside me somewhere in the bushes, possibly chasing a rabbit. I was warning bears, rapists, and murderers that I was not alone. But I was.

At the elementary school where this trail began, I could have instead taken the smooth asphalt trail that paralleled the road. Instead, I chose the steep dirt and gravel path through the woods and down to the creek. On this summer Friday evening, when the sun would never truly set, my husband was out of town, my daughter was grown and just fine on her own, my grandkids were away on their own adventures, and I had deliberately made no plans to spend time with friends.

Biking was the only cure for this pent-up energy that had been buzzing in my body during a day spent sitting in front of my computer at work, boxed in, writing reports, sending emails, wishing I were retired, while the few good days of summer weather slipped away.

I thought I'd have more company in my solitude, though, that I'd pass some other bikers or dog walkers or joggers on these back trails. Where was everyone on such a lovely summer's night? Had there been a bear mauling recently I didn't hear about? Not far from here, a year ago, a young girl was mauled by a brown bear during an all-night bike race. Near the same location that same season another runner, not in a race, was also attacked. Both women lived to tell about it, but experienced lasting physical and emotional scars. In addition, I couldn't forget that a few years ago I had found a chunk of shredded moose hide and hair—evidence a bear had killed a moose close by—while hiking on the trail I was now descending. I savored my solitude, but did I really want to be all alone on the trail? I craved my independence yet horrified myself when I grabbed it.

"Pay attention!" I whispered, forcing my focus to the ground in front of me as I tried to steer my bike toward the least rocky route on this long downhill ride to the creek. I swerved to miss a big spruce root. My fingers ached from squeezing the brakes. If I spun out or teakettled over a pothole, there was no one near to pick up the pieces. "Here, Dirk," I yelled to my imaginary companion.

It took all my concentration to stay upright and avoid catastrophe. I was a late-blooming biker. My family—husband, daughter, son-in-law and grandkids—bought me my first bike for Mother's Day four years ago. "Go Mema!" my grandkids said, the name they've always called me.

"No girl of mine is going to ride a bike," my dad had declared when I was young. "She might get herself killed."

I secretly learned to ride my friend's brother's bike at age twelve. Though other kids tossed insults at the big girl riding the little bike, the humiliation was worth it when feet, peddles, balance, and determination all worked in harmony and I coasted to freedom down the dusty, rutted alley. For the next forty-years I had rarely gotten on a bike. I rented one on vacation once, and occasionally borrowed one from a friend, but this plum-colored beauty was my first truly new, this-is-my-own bike.

My neck bounced, vertebrae colliding, wiping out all my hard-earned progress in Rolfing and Pilates. I wondered if this jostling was good for my brain. On my job I taught people about shaken-baby syndrome. What about shaken-lady syndrome? I wobbled at the start of any ride and I usually shifted at the wrong time, winding up walking the bike up long hills. Occasionally, I biked with the grandkids and Jim, always in the back of the pack, taking my time. On one of those outings, not far from where I was going this day, Jim broke away to do a short, single-track loop with the kids while I stayed on the wider main trail. As I waited for them at the next fork, the kids came rushing back on their bikes saying, "Papa crashed!" Jim had hit a root, flown over his handlebars, and landed on his helmet and shoulder. As I peddled behind the kids to find out where he was, imagining how to explain our location to the paramedics, we found him limping beside his bike, helmet askew, visor broken off from the front. After X-rays and an MRI, we learned he required extensive surgery to patch and pin the shoulder back together. As I clumped down the hill, pulling hard on the brakes, I knew I did not want that to happen to me.

Yet when I strapped on my helmet, slipped on my fluorescent green reflecting vest, and pulled on my bike gloves, I imagined myself an athlete, a woman as fit as the skinny young students who hitched their bikes to the same rack I did at the university where I worked.

The trail leveled out and my bike clunked to a stop on the hefty wooden bridge across the creek. This was a multi-use trail: walkers, bikers, joggers, and horses in summer; skiers, and snowshoers in winter; and dogs all year long. Oh, and moose, bears, coyotes, and an occasional lynx whenever they were so inclined.

I leaned my bike against the wooden railing, took a long swig from my water bottle, and gazed into the creek. At that moment the water ran clear, undisturbed by dogs or curious kids mucking up the sandy bottom. Last spring I brought Cason and Carly down here during break-up. They jumped on the edges of the rotten ice, threw rocks and sticks in the water, and generally got thoroughly soaked and filthy—but tired and proud of themselves.

This creek and I had come to know each other well during the twenty-five years we had shared the same neighborhood. Once you could spot tiny Dolly Varden trout right here at the bridge when the sandy bottom was still. But now they were rare. With all the subdivisions and culverts down below, the fish couldn't make it up here to spawn. Jim and I had planned to have our wedding ceremony here beside this creek, but it was too far for my parents to walk and the mosquitoes would have attacked us mercilessly.

Just when I was ready to turn around and return the way I had come, having avoided any bears or perverts, a young couple strode briskly up to the bridge from the other direction with their panting black lab in tow. The old dog lifted his head, perked up, and dashed for the creek, where he plunked down and lapped the cool water.

"Seen any big animals out there?" I asked.

"No. Just us," the woman replied.

Surely, I reasoned, they had swept the trail ahead clear of dangerous creatures. I shoved off from the bridge, teetering at first until my cranky knees loosened up and I finally reached an upright rhythm. I sped up for the wide-open stretch of trail I could see ahead. I let my mind wander. My shadow raced beside me in the alders, the twelve-year-old girl I'd left behind.

Chapter Thirteen

Denali National Park, Teklanika River, 1973

I was a twenty-six-year-old adult—and four months pregnant—the first time I visited Denali National Park. Then it was called McKinley National Park, named after a president who had never even set foot in Alaska let alone viewed the mountain.

Why would a kid raised in Alaska wait so long to visit the state's most famous national park? "Not worth the trouble," said my father. "Too far away and too many rules."

The park *was* over two million acres (which was expanded to a total of six million acres in 1980), and before the paved two-lane Parks Highway was completed in 1971, a trip to Denali meant a 250-mile drive north from Anchorage to Paxson, then another 135 miles across the notoriously rutted gravel road called the Denali Highway, then another thirty miles just to the park entrance. Before 1972, visitors were allowed to travel the one-lane gravel park road its entire ninety miles to the old Kantishna mining area if the vehicles had high clearance and the drivers had nerves of steel. The road had drop-offs with no guard rails or shoulders. Dad had no stomach for that kind of adventure when he could fish and camp much closer to town.

By the time of my first trip, visitors could only drive the first fifteen miles of the road, the rest of the park only reachable by bus. My first husband Ron and I, since returning to Alaska after college, had taken little time to explore the homeland to which we longed to return in our year of wandering. This trip was our chance to get back into the wild country we both loved before the baby was born. I was healthy and strong and determined pregnancy would not slow me down. We packed up everything we would need for a three-day backcountry trip in Denali.

Once inside the park, Ron and I pitched our tent the first night at the Riley Creek campground, accessible by car, near the park entrance. We hiked the trails near the park headquarters, the only formal trails there at that time. The next morning we set out to catch a park bus into the backcountry. (I don't remember needing a permit then.) We shouldered our backpacks, waited at the bus stop for one of the retired school buses that served as a backcountry shuttle, rode for a couple of hours, then disembarked at the bridge over the Teklanika River, a braided gray glacial river. On our bus ride, with the help of the keen eyes of the driver and fellow passengers, we spotted moose, caribou, foxes, dozens of ground squirrels, and a grizzly with cubs digging up roots in the tundra.

As we climbed down the stairs of the bus and it pulled away, we stood by ourselves overlooking the river. Bears were on my mind. Descending from the road to the river bar, I was aware of the life I was now responsible for, and how we had stepped out of our comfortable urban life into a world in which we were not the dominant creatures. No trails here, no signs marking our route, no other hikers in view, the bridge and road growing smaller as we plodded beside the river. It had been two years since we had last backpacked, down the Grand Canyon to the Colorado River. That trail, though steep and strenuous, teemed with people and felt anything but wild. Now my pack felt heavier and my balance less stable, my feet stumbling in the glacial sand and rounded rocks. We had hoped to see Denali, the High One, as the Native people had named it, but it had not yet appeared. We could sense its presence though, in the weather, the volatile mix of dark clouds, rain squalls, and shafts of sunlight.

Constantly scanning the willows for bears, we discovered signs of their presence—mounds of dirt and gravel they had excavated in search of succulent roots below, piles of scat full of seeds and berries. Despite the wilderness woman I wanted to be, I was terrified of bears. Commercial bear sprays were not yet on the market, nor bear-proof backpacking food containers. Memories of bear stories I had grown up hearing—surprise charges; maulings; rogue, human-eating bears—tore through my imagination. It didn't matter this was decades before the first (and so far only) fatal bear attack in Denali Park.

In addition, there was another obstacle to confront. According to the ranger we consulted before we left the visitor center, we learned we would have to cross several braids in the river along our planned journey. He explained how and when to safely cross a glacial river—wait until early morning or late at night when the melt water from the glaciers is at its lowest ebb, choose a wide, shallower branch, unhook your pack in case you slip and fall into the river, brace yourself with a stout stick, ease across slowly, be prepared to quickly lose sensation in your feet and legs in the icy flow. It sounded both simple and treacherous.

We followed the river until our backs and feet begged for respite, then pitched camp on the gravel bar, against the constant roar of the river. We heated freeze-dried food on our temperamental one-burner backpacking stove, then searched for a place to stash our bag of food away from camp. There were no trees to throw a rope over and hoist our food out of reach of bears, so we placed the food bag on a flat rock several minutes' walk from our tent. To warn the bears humans were around, we tied a metal cup, fork, and spoon to a stick and jammed it between rocks in hopes it would clang in the breeze. A pathetic defense, but something. Buried in my sleeping bag inside the tent that night, I lay awake listening to the distant tinkle of utensils in the wind, sure a bear was stealing our food, before heading to eat us.

The next day we walked and walked but found nowhere to cross. It was peak pollen season in the park, and pregnancy seemed to magnify my allergies. I endured fits of explosive sneezing, itchy and weeping eyes, a gushing nose, and fiery sinuses, yet refrained from taking my allergy medication because my doctor cautioned me not to take it unless absolutely necessary.

My wilderness bravado collided with my human frailty and nature's indifference. We approached the river's edge again and again, searching for a wide shallow spot to cross, but the current ran so fast and the water was so murky we could not tell the depth. We reached a decision point, blocked finally by the river channel we had been following. Cross or turn back? We studied the current and scouted for riffles indicating a shallower depth, but found none. "Let's turn around," said Ron, eager to head back to the road, shed his backpack, and reach a safe campground with people. "No," I said, with a determination I didn't really feel, "let's wait until tonight and see if the river comes down," Tears and snot ran down my face as I tried to breathe through my allergic reaction. I was miserable, a long way from the woman who promised she would not let pregnancy slow her down. "You should turn around," Ron said.

I did not want to admit defeat, but at least now I could blame him for the decision. I gave in and swallowed an allergy pill, and prayed my baby would survive this trip and grow to be more courageous than her mother.

Denali National Park, Igloo Creek, 1982

I brought my eight-year-old daughter Elisha to Denali because I wanted her to experience the park earlier than I did. I wanted her to fall in love with the tundra, the animals, the wide valleys, the glaciers, and, if we got to see it, the mountain itself. Elisha, Jim, and I camped in one small tent at the Igloo Creek Campground at Mile 34 of the park road. We waited at the campground bus stop to venture deeper into the park. The day was dreary, Elisha was bored, and the mosquitoes tortured us. Not knowing how long before the next bus arrived, we crossed the road and headed toward Igloo Mountain. Slogging through the willows we yelled, "Hey, bear!" to announce our presence and found a social trail—unofficial, but well used—that led out of the brush to higher ground. I did not intend to climb to the top of the mountain, just a quick diversion from our wait for the bus. We reached tree line. Far enough for me. I announced I was ready to turn around.

"Let's go higher and find some sheep," said Jim.

Elisha stuck with him. Steadily up the slope. Leaving me behind. Soft tundra gave way to scree—sharp, loose rocks. With each step I slid down a few inches, stones raking my ankles. Loose rocks were my most terrifying challenge on a steep slope. I froze when I should have kept moving. I could not erase the image in my mind of one of us lying at the bottom of the slope, head sliced open. But they ignored me, husband and daughter a team now, climbing higher and higher while I stepped slowly, urging myself on with shaky legs and trembling heart. We reached a narrow chute: larger rocks, packed dirt. Jim and Elisha tackled it ahead of me, squeezed through, feet and hands hoisting, hauling, propelling their bodies up and up until they reached a narrow ridge. I froze in place, not sure where to step, where to put my hands. Jim called down: *Step there, hold on there, grab this, grab that.*

Elisha cheered me on.

"You can make it, Mom."

When did our roles become reversed? Finally I reached solid rock. But it offered scant security because the slope fell away sharply on either side. Together again, we kept climbing until we were at the top, below us the gray ribbon of park road on one side, a flock of Dall mountain sheep grazing on the other, Igloo Creek coursing its many channels in the slate-colored gravel bar. In her triumph of reaching the top, Elisha turned cartwheels on the dragon-spine of the mountain. My heart skittered as I watched her cavorting on the spine's sharp edge. Sure-footed and courageous, I had produced a mountain sheep in spite of myself.

***

Denali State Park, 1987, Kesugi Ridge

The serrated ridge taunted, so close. Jim, Elisha, and I were camped at Byer's Lake, in Denali State Park, a hundred miles south of Denali National Park,

A dash to the top to take in the view, a glimpse of the valley on the far side, a quick retreat down the slope. Elisha would never be out of sight. I could do this. I had to do it.

From above, the gray granite boulder where we left Elisha appeared flat and short, less tower than altar. Perched on top, she curled knees to chest, still and exposed, the green inflatable brace around her ankle bulging like a tire about to burst. The doctor said walking would be good for her ankle as long as she wore the air cast to keep it from twisting.

I pushed hard and fast up the mountain. Each time I glanced back, Elisha looked smaller and smaller. It was hard to know when a stubborn child tells the truth or simply wants her own way. She was tired, she said. Her ankle hurt. I urged her on. She slumped down on a patch of dwarf willow.

I wanted her to love hiking, camping, all things outdoors, but at age twelve a daughter begins to undo the knot that ties her to her mother. Her mother tugs back, yet secretly longs to be free. She was a wiry child. Somersaults, cartwheels, splits, parallel bars, balance beams. Leotards, ponytails, tiny breasts. Practices, performances, applause. With one spectacular backwards flip, it ended.

A shattered ankle. A year of pins and wire, grafts, casts and crutches. Medals, accolades, the exhilaration of a perfect performance, gone. She would be no gymnast.

In that same year I decided to trade soft, flowing skirts

for gray pinstripes and a corporate paycheck, to trade a job helping people for a job helping the bottom line. In that same year, my daughter hobbled one-legged to and from the bus stop through the snow because I could not get time off from work. The job was that important, the life I'd dreamed of just within reach, a good paycheck, steady work that didn't involve helping broken families.

She managed three miles up the mountain, along a raggedy lake trail, across a wavy slip of a bridge, through the inside-out umbrella-shaped cow parsnips waving higher than she stood, past a roaring cascade of icy water, and up, up above tree line. The crest, so impossible at the start, lay at last within reach.

That's when she refused to go any farther. But our trail was a bear highway marked by old washed-out signs and fresh brown mounds filled with berries. Sometimes I pushed too hard, but I wasn't the kind of mother to leave her child for bait.

Jim suggested the rock. She'd be safe there, he said. My legs tingled, and I began to shiver in the breeze. Elisha ripped a patch of moss from the ground and stared down at the green oval lake at the bottom of the trail. "I don't care what you do," she said, "I'm not going any farther."

S*he didn't need me. She didn't even want me around*, I reasoned.

"We may never get this far again," said Jim the wanderer.

She could rest. I could reach the summit. We'd both get our way. She said nothing as we boosted her up the steep, grainy side of the boulder, then handed her a backpack and placed the bear spray beside her.

The quicker I put distance between us, the sooner I would be on my way down. As the tundra thinned to glacial rubble,

I made myself look forward, not back. Stacks of lichen-covered rocks marked the way, cairns that stretched toward the thickening clouds. The elusive ridge seemed more and more distant. Blasting across the empty landscape, wind raked grit across my face. My calves, knees, thighs, and heart labored together as the trail grew steeper, stonier, more difficult. An exhilarating burst of freedom, I told myself.

The sky darkened as clouds closed in. Against my firmest resolve, I glanced back. No boulder. No daughter. She was gone from my sight. Now there was no ridge, no summit, no goal. I envisioned splattered blood, shredded clothes, bits of bone, and clumps of hair. My only child, my love, my heart. I deserted her. How could I be so selfish?

I called to Jim, then pivoted, stumbled, and lurched back down the mountain, past one cairn, then another, and another. Rain pelted the rocks, greasing the uneven cobbles as clouds sheeted with gray began to close around me. Now there was just the rocky path that led me back to the little girl I had left alone.

Boots skidding, I slipped, caught myself, continued. At last it came into view, near and sure, the flat stone surface, the small X of feet, legs, arms, the head hidden beneath a yellow raincoat.

As I reached the rock, a head of matted blond hair popped out from beneath the raincoat.

"Back so soon?" she asked.

I tried to crawl up but the stone was slick, and I scraped my knee sliding down. She eased to the edge and jumped off, landing on her good foot. Our hug was brief and sopping. "You stink, Mom," she said.

I let go of her, exhausted, relieved. "I love you."

"Yeah." She shifted, putting distance between us. "I'm hungry."

I fetched a smashed granola bar from my pack, a small offering. Clouds bunched at the summit, jagged and bare. It was raining there too. I could see it from here.

Chapter Fourteen

She stood alone in the spotlight in the middle of the hard, cold ice rink. The red tutu and the matching ribbons spiraling down the back of her tightly curled hair added neither height nor breadth to her tiny form. I bit my lip and applauded along with family and strangers as the music began, a tinkling of notes from a vaguely familiar movie tune, and she bravely shoved off. Arms wide, legs steady, she circled the rink with quick, confident strides, then wiggled backwards to the center of the rink, shook her hips, pirouetted, and bowed to the judges.

The music continued, violins rising to a crescendo, but she had already stopped. She scanned the crowd, her expression shifting from joy to confusion as she tried to fathom how her perfect routine somehow galloped ahead of the song. She burst into sobs and scurried off the rink, a shaken and deflated two-year-old.

Six years and dozens of performances later, I still gnashed my teeth and clenched my fists when my granddaughter

Carly, took the spotlight on the ice. I followed her every move, praying she would not fall, break a limb, collapse from anxiety, or crumble in defeat. With every performance I rooted for a happy ending. I groaned when any skater crashed while doing a leap or spiral, knowing next time it could be Carly, even though she had never fallen in a performance.

Her anxious eyes, her frozen smile—I dreamed these would dissolve into joy if she and I could only take to the ice, grandmother and granddaughter together, on a lake, wind tingling our cheeks, legs pumping, ankles straight and strong, having nothing but fun. If I were with her instead of only watching. But for Carly's family—her brother, mother, and dad—ice time is not about wind-tingled cheeks or side-by-side skating or laughter. Ice time is serious business.

Both my grandkids laced up their first skates—or rather their parents laced them up for them—as soon as they could stand. Their dad presented Cason, Carly's older brother, with his first hockey stick at the age of six months. By age three Cason had joined his first hockey "team," a clutch of flailing tykes scrambling to locate the puck, on his way to fulfilling his Dad's dreams for him: a place on a competitive youth hockey team, then a high school varsity team, and maybe even in a professional junior league. At age ten, Cason practiced two or three times a week during hockey season, depending on how much ice time his team could wrangle. In addition, he worked with an individual coach before school two days a week and played one or two games a week against rivals, not counting tournaments. Carly too had her own hefty schedule, with her own coach and choreographer.

When I was a kid, I skated for fun. There were no indoor ice rinks, but there was an outdoor rink at each grade school.

You brought your skates to school so you could do something more interesting at recess than stand around shivering or losing a wool mitten to the frozen monkey bars.

I learned to skate at six, not at the school, but with my dad on Lake Spenard. There the only competitors for ice time were the small ski planes that used the lake as a winter runway. After freeze-up, neighbors shoveled the snow off a small area clear of the taxiway. Someone would stack wood and build a warm-up fire on shore. Childhood was a less structured experience then. Kids were sent out to play, and told to stay out of trouble and be home for dinner.

Our town now supports six indoor ice arenas, each with two rinks. They all have the same concrete floors, concrete block walls, dirty white tiles, beat-up backboards, Plexiglas shields, nets to catch stray pucks that sail over the glass, and restrooms you don't want to use except in an emergency. But the ice is always perfect, smoothed and pampered between each group by an elegant and efficient motorized god, the Zamboni. Figure skaters compete with hockey teams for ice time, and hockey teams compete with each other. All pay dearly for their chance to slice the ice.

The yearly cost to keep Cason in competitive hockey easily equaled the cost of a year of college at our state university (around $6,000 at the time). This didn't count travel expenses to games in other towns (and sometimes even other states). Then add the cost of Carly's figure skating, with her own coach, her ice time, her practice jackets and leggings, her frilly costumes, her accompanying hats and hair bands and flesh-colored tights, plus travel to her competitions, and you've totaled the equivalent of another collegiate semester. And ice time demands more than money. It requires devotion—time, energy, and focus. Skating is more than a sport. It's a way of life, an extended family. Carpools, raffles to raise money, hockey games, days and nights on the road with skaters and parents and coaches. I admired the dedication of my daughter and son-in-law, their commitment to the kids' sports.

I taught Cason and Carly's mother to skate at her elementary school rink. I was a frazzled single mom living in a tiny house in a neighborhood of boxy flat-roofed homes within arm's reach of each other. At night, exhausted after a day of dealing with troubled families at the counseling center where I worked then, I'd bundle Elisha up, slide her little feet into a pair of figure skates, load her on a sled, and haul her to the school. When we reached the outdoor rink, she'd jump from the sled and circle the ice while I sat on the sled and squeezed my feet into my own scuffed-up skates, lacing them quickly before my fingers were too stiff to move. We'd skate until our toes grew numb, then head home for hot chocolate. I cherished those skating excursions, before Jim and I moved in together, before we changed neighborhoods and Elisha changed schools, before she became a brooding adolescent. I hoped her memories of those times were as happy as mine.

Our mother-daughter enchantment ended too quickly. In middle school, Elisha's longings reached beyond the ice rink. She begged me to let her try downhill skiing. I don't know where she got the idea—a friend, a teacher, a need to break away from me perhaps. Showing a fearless nature I lacked, she happily signed up for ski school. Every Saturday for weeks I packed her lunch, kissed her goodbye, and put her on the ski bus. I had tried to master downhill skiing myself before she was born, the memory of my failed attempt with Dad so long ago still etched in my brain. But as an adult, one stunning plummet down the mountain, followed by a ride in the ski patrol basket, convinced me to give it up.

I took up cross-country skis instead. No lifts, no terrifying plunges down a mountain, just the rhythmic slide of one foot, then the other. I learned easily. Flat terrain, deep snow, rolling hills, groomed trails—I could cover ground. Dad would have been proud. With the right wax I could have coasted down that hill behind our little rented house with ease. When no-wax skis came out, I bought a pair with fish scales on the bottoms, eliminating the guesswork on applying the right wax for the specific temperature and conditions. Those reliable skis carried me through the years—a new marriage, a daughter grown and gone, the births of two grandchildren.

Meanwhile, a new style of cross-country skiing was becoming popular. Developed for racing, skate skiing required more skill, effort, and precision than the classic method. I admired the flowing side-to-side dance of the young skate skiers who whisked past me while I shuffled along on a parallel track. I wanted to feel that kind of freedom, skate-skiing.

On one particularly soggy August morning, I divided my time between two cold, cavernous, dingy, echoing ice rinks, bundled in winter gear, perched on metal bleachers until my hip joints screamed and I lost feeling in my butt. My daughter couldn't deliver the kids to two places at once, so she had asked for help while her husband Chad worked his twenty-four-hour shift at the fire department. She drove eight-year-old Carly twenty miles to a figure skating competition while I chauffeured ten-year-old Cason to hockey practice.

Rain puddled in the grimy parking lot as Cason and I arrived at the sports complex. He lugged his gear toward the locker room as I faded into the background with the rest of the parents and grandparents who chatted, drank coffee, and texted on their cell phones. The locker room was off-limits to family. When Cason was younger, I was allowed into the inner sanctum to help lace his skates. Now the coach wanted no distractions while he preached strategy, motivation, and concentration. I was happy to stay outside. The locker room was noisy and crowded; it smelled of sweat and mold and there was no clean place to stand.

Hockey was a foreign language to me, one I was painfully slow to learn. I knew only that one team must slam the black plastic disc into the other team's net. To do this, players must skate very fast. A puck sounds like a gunshot when crashed against the sideboards. And when a player gets hurt, he tries his best not to cry.

While I didn't pretend to understand the rules *on* the rink, the ones *off* the rink were clear, for me, at least. As much as possible, remain invisible. When picking him up from practice, never touch, move, ask questions about, or offer to carry any piece of hockey gear. Attendance at games was allowed—in fact, expected—but no hugs, kisses, or physical contact before or after the game. High fives, handshakes, or pats on top of his ball cap were sometimes allowed if his team won, but absolutely no congratulatory hugs.

While training for figure skating is a dance, hockey practice is preparing for war. Kids stream in wearing baseball caps and tennis shoes, hauling big boxy nylon bags on their scrawny shoulders. Minutes later they emerge ready for battle—taller, straighter, wider, with masked faces and helmeted heads. Pass. Receive. Pass. They weave in and around each other, sweeping the ice with their sticks. I searched for Cason among the swirl of gray, black, and blue snaking around the ice. He had a certain way of thrusting his head slightly forward, of swaying back and forth, of making quick little sweeps with his stick as he zipped down the rink. Weeks had passed since I had last watched him practice. He skated with more speed now. More grace. More determination. He slapped the puck like he meant it.

I admired Cason and Carly—their focus, their determination, their faith in their own abilities. It was more than I had at their age.

After hockey practice, Cason and I headed for his sister's figure skating competition. "I don't want to watch a bunch of dumb figure skaters," he grumbled. "It's boring."

"But she comes to your hockey games," I replied.

"I don't care."

I admit figure skating lacked the quick-paced action of hockey. Each skater performed two routines—one freestyle, one artistic. Carly was given a place on the performance schedule, grouped by experience level. Each routine required a specified length of time. For Carly's group, this meant one hundred agonizing seconds on the ice. Skaters warmed up, performed their solos, then exited the ice while the judges debated each score. Unlike the Olympics, no one knew the winner until an hour or two after each performance. It required a lot of perseverance to wait for the person you love to perform, then a lot of stomach-churning and nail-biting while you waited for her score to be posted. For Cason, after the exertion and excitement of his hockey practice, a figure skating competition was nothing but dead time. No guys to talk to, nothing to watch but a bunch of nervous girls fluttering around in and out of the locker rooms, now off-limits to him, nothing to do but plop on a bleacher and pilfer a treat from the figure-skaters' snack table.

Sometimes I wondered if Carly's real love was not figure skating, but her skating coach of six years—the lithe, lovely, red-haired Savanna. Carly might have been a cranky, complaining little girl when I picked her up at school for her skating lesson, but by the time she crossed the rink to Savanna's side, she had transformed into a beaming, cooperative, attentive student. As she and Savanna cruised the rink doing warm-up laps, I glimpsed a trace of myself basking in the fleeting gaze of my handsome young father so many years back. With no desire for solo performances, Dad and I were a skating team. I yearned for Carly's grace and courage and, if I was honest, for a sliver of the admiration she bestowed upon Savanna.

Cason and I arrived a few minutes before Carly's second performance. As a sullen Cason sat on the bench, I entered the figure skaters' locker room where the lingering smell of sweat from previous hockey players was overlain with the sweet, sticky smells of multiple brands of hairspray and glittery make-up. This was a world of flesh-colored tights, gauze, sequins, sculpted hair, dark eyes, red cheeks, and ruby lips. Carly's mom gave her hair one more spray and twisted the strands of a silver headband into place.

"Okay. Okay." Carly winced and waved her mom back. I stood to the side, gathering stray pieces of clothing to stuff into Carly's wheeled skating bag.

"I know you'll do your best, sweetie," I mumbled, and kissed her stiff hair.

"Go get 'em," Elisha said, brushing Carly's cheek with a kiss.

Carly pulled away and headed out the locker room door. I knew from experience Carly's fear and anxiety usually took the form of anger, directed at the people closest to her. Elisha and I gathered the rest of the debris scattered on the locker room sink, climbed up the bleacher steps to get a good view, and sat down.

When her long-awaited turn came, Carly floated onto the vast white expanse of ice. Tall for her age, in a pink sequined costume, she was a wisp of cotton candy on her long, thin legs. To win, all must be synchronized—her music, her moves, her timing—none of the disastrous flub that befell her at age two. Her routine had to be embedded in her muscle fibers and executed perfectly. She had to believe she would rather be on this icy platform in front of these critical eyes than anywhere else on earth.

She pushed off as the music began. She swirled and twirled and swooped, claiming the cold, empty space as her own, skates flashing as she executed the routine she had prepared for so many hours, days, and months. Her routine ended in complete synchrony with the music as she coasted to the judges' platform and bowed, flushed and triumphant.

She exited the ice as Elisha and I scrambled from the bleachers to congratulate her, proud to have witnessed her hard-earned moments of perfection. She was the skater of my childhood dreams. I hugged her cold, bony body to my waist.

"Perfect!" I said as Elisha handed her a jacket and Carly tottered off on her pink skate guards to watch the rest of the skaters. An hour later, during which Cason joined us and complained continually of boredom, the judges posted the scores from Carly's group. We scurried to the message board to read the scrap of paper. Carly took second place. Tears puddled in her eyes as she gathered her medal from where it sat on the folding table, slipped it over her head, and stepped onto the platform to pose for a picture with Savanna.

"Next time." Savanna whispered. "That girl was older."

Carly straightened, smeared her mascara-streaked face on Savanna's jacket, and smiled.

Cason, urged by his mother, handed his sister a stuffed toy puppy and gave her a grudging hug. We gathered her gear and walked to the parking lot under clear skies and the evening sun.

"Thanks, Mom." Elisha hugged my neck.

"Sure," I said. We transferred Cason's bulky hockey bag from my car to hers. They pulled away. I waved goodbye and climbed into my car. For the long trip home, I rode alone.

It had been years since I'd been on the ice. Ankles laced in leather, blades scritching across the rough surface of a frozen lake, cheeks burning in the wind. But those flashes lodged deep in my memory, flawless moments with my dad beside me, snow flying, making me feel as if I were the most beautiful girl in the world, the most gifted, the most free.

I wondered what Carly would remember of this day, of this season, of these years at the rink. Of her grandmother, watching from the stands, dreaming not of medals and trophies but of gliding beside her, sharing the ice.

Chapter Fifteen

Those days I was mostly a chauffeur.

I arrived at the rink to pick Cason up from another hockey practice. He dumped his hockey sticks and bag into the back of my car.

"How did practice go?"

"Okay"

"How was school today?"

"Okay."

"How's your science project going?"

"Why are you asking me so many questions?" he barked.

"I'm interested in what you're doing."

"I don't want to talk about it."

Dismissal. Condescension. Sarcasm. He wouldn't talk to his dad like this, I reasoned, or his Papa Jim. Memories of arrogant men from my past appeared suddenly, those that interrupted, talked over me, cut off conversation, refused to listen. Co-workers, bosses, friends, my ex-husband.

How dare you talk to me like that? I wanted to scream.

Instead, I took a few measured breaths. Maybe practice went badly, or school, or something else.

"I don't care if you're cranky," is what finally came out. "Don't be rude to me."

Of course my grandson would not grow into the kind of man who acts like he's better than women. He would be sensitive and caring. I'd make sure of it. But how? I knew nothing about raising teenage boys.

Maybe I expected too much, maybe I was over-involved, maybe I missed the easy conversations of his early years. Besides, my daughter Elisha and her husband Chad were doing a fine job raising their kids. I had no grandparent role models, given my dad's parents had died in the car accident on the Alaska Highway when I was six, and the other set lived 3,000 miles away.

Two weeks later we were back in the car, again on the way to hockey practice. I made another stab at small talk.

"What do you want for your birthday?" I asked.

"I'll text you my list."

"For godsakes, we're here in the car! Just tell me."

"Okay. I want a dirt bike. A video camera I can stick on my handlebars to record my jumps. And a .22 rifle."

"A gun?"

His mom wouldn't even let him have toy guns, and .22s, though rarely lethal, can cause serious damage to the human body. She'd never take that risk.

"Why do you want a gun?"

"So I can go hunting."

"Your dad doesn't hunt."

"I'll hunt with my friends and their dads."

An opening here. A chance to impress and connect with

the boy I no longer had much in common with.

"I used to hunt," I told him.

He leaned closer and turned to face me.

"*You* used to go hunting?"

"Birds. I used to hunt birds." He had only known me in the bird-*watching* phase of my life. "With your other grandpa," I said, meaning Ron, my ex-husband. "He hunted ducks. You had to get up early." What I remember mostly is the cold. The darkness. Everything wet. How we sat freezing in the swamp, waiting for the birds to fly so we could shoot at them. How the gun tore into my shoulder every time I fired it. I only lasted one season, but didn't tell Cason that.

"What kind of gun did you use?" he asks.

"A shotgun."

"What kind?"

"I don't remember."

The discussion ended as abruptly as it had begun.

I remembered the Fourth of July celebration a few weeks earlier at my daughter's cabin on Nancy Lake. (Growing tired of the lack of water and sewer at the family cabin—and the inability of my sisters to contribute financially to improvements—Chad and Elisha had bought their own cabin on Nancy Lake from the parents of one of their high school friends. It was a sturdy two-story structure, with sewer, running water, garage, a large deck, and a dock—a second home, really.) The Fourth was a cool, overcast day, with just enough breeze to frustrate the mosquitoes. Chad grilled ribs and chicken while Cason, perched on a tall metal chair, was surrounded by men—friends of his parents and neighbors from other cabins. As I carted salads, breads, and hot dishes from the kitchen to the serving table outside, I overheard bits of their conversations. They were talking guns. Pistols, rifles, antique guns, expensive guns, collections of guns so rare they had to be locked away in secret places. Cason's eyes widened, tracking each speaker, smiling slightly, nodding in silence. When I returned from the grill with a plate of ribs, the conversation had turned to hunting. Trophies mounted on walls. Trophies they hoped to pursue. As I caught the smile on Cason's face I was uneasy, not about hunting, but about his fascination with gun talk, with men who kill for sport, who treat animals like trophies. This is not the kind of hunting I was raised with, to kill simply for sport, for one's own ego. This is not the kind of man I wanted Cason to be; I wanted him to respect animals and value the beauty of the natural world we were lucky enough have around us.

Here in Alaska lots of people owned guns. When hunting season opened, there was a migration of hunters from towns and villages to the woods and tundra in search of moose, caribou, and other game. When I was growing up, our family lived all winter on the animals my father killed—meat butchered and wrapped by my mother and aunt on our kitchen table. Even now, my husband kept a shotgun stored in our closet at home, for back country bear protection.

Though Cason's dad didn't seem interested in hunting or guns, there were plenty of good men in his world who owned guns and used them safely. Hard-working, support-your-family hockey dads. Men who sat for hours on metal benches at frigid ice rinks, attended back-to-school nights, helped with homework, hauled their daughters to volleyball practice, cooked meals for their families, took their sick kids to the hospital. Men to look up to. Their family friend Rob was one of those men. Fun, hard-working, successful, church-going, willing to support his wife in developing her own business. On the few times our paths crossed he always greeted me with warmth and interest.

A few days after the birthday discussion, I brought Carly to one of the ice rinks for figure skating practice. Rob sat on the bleachers while his daughter, Carly's age, finished her lesson. The girls shared the same skating coach. Rob's son was on Cason's hockey team. The boys were best buddies, the families traveled and camped together, and gathered to celebrate birthdays and holidays. Just two weeks ago the boys and their dads spent a weekend racing through the muck and rain on their dirt bikes while the moms and girls hung out in the shelter of a motorhome. I envied the friendship of the two families, raising their kids in tandem. As a single mother raising Elisha, I had few friends with children to spend time with.

Climbing up onto the bleachers I spotted Rob sitting a few benches below me. He turned to look at me briefly but said nothing. I pointed to the overhead heaters that sporadically radiated warm air on spectators.

"Heat?" I asked Rob.

"Not that I can tell," he said. Then he turned to stare at the empty rink his daughter had just left. He seemed preoccupied and, without saying goodbye, left as soon as she traded skates for tennis shoes.

A few weeks later, Jim and I arrived at Elisha's house to celebrate Cason's thirteenth birthday. Dolly, their small white Westie, greeted us at the door by jumping on our legs. The smell of pizza permeated the house as we took off our shoes and set Cason's presents on the table by the living room window. He had already opened the presents from his sister and parents, and was excited to show us one of them. He gestured into the kitchen where several cartons of pizza and a birthday cake with hockey sticks and pucks waited for us on the counter. A long black case sat on the kitchen table. He unlatched it and opened the lid. Against a purple velvet lining lay a .22 caliber rifle. Like a finely crafted piece of furniture, the stock was warm brown, smooth and polished, carved with delicate cross-hatching. Cason beamed as he ran his fingers across the spine of the gun, lingering over the unblemished wood, the gleaming barrel.

"How nice," I said. I pictured carcasses of small animals and birds littering the woods near the family's cabin. Shattered windows. Splintered trees. Worse yet, a stray bullet stuck in his sister's eye. Jim accused me of always imagining the worst. Maybe he was right. Elisha assured me Cason would take a gun safety class and shoot only while at the firing range. But I still didn't understand why he wanted a gun. I worried he took this too lightly, this business of killing—so easy, so thrilling, so clean in the video games he played with his friends. Or maybe a gun was simply an object to mark his entrance into the world of men, a sign of independence. I wished there were better ways to mark this rite of passage. I realized how little influence I had over his life compared to the culture around us. What could a bird-watching grandma from a long-ago era offer that was more thrilling than firing a gun, or following celebrities on social media, or listening to the X-rated lyrics of hip-hop music? We were a society fixated on youth, with technologies moving faster than anyone could follow, finding little need for wisdom or contribution from a previous generation.

Chapter Sixteen

In the fifteen years since you died, Joe, we returned to Denver three times to throw out more of your stuff, and we're still not done. The garage, the old chicken coop, the porch, the carport, the yard, and now behind this hidden door in the belly of the cellar. Your work clothes, hung where you left them, drooping from hooks like deflated bodies. Coveralls, overalls, shirts, sweaters. Filthy, paint-spattered, and full of holes. I didn't want to touch them, but I had to.

I wanted to be done with you, Joe. Wash my hands, run out of this house, empty my mind of you.

I jerked a heavy brown sweater from its hook, sending an explosion of dust up my nose and across my tee shirt. I dropped the crumbling bundle of wool into the trash. I pictured my father-in-law wagging his fat, callused finger at me, demanding to know what I was doing with his stuff. Good question. I had no desire to sort through a lifetime of crap belonging to someone I barely knew and had tried my best to avoid. *Some things just can't be saved, Joe.*

***

After Joe died I began to appreciate and love Jim's mother, Lucille. She would welcome us into her home and tell stories about her family's mortuary business in Spaulding, Nebraska, and how she and her sisters had moved to the big city of Denver to find work because her brother, as the only male in the family, took over the business, excluding them. She accepted Elisha as a step-grandchild and didn't seem to care whether we went to church or if Jim and I got an annulment.

For Lucille's ninetieth birthday, we helped Jim's brother Paul organize a huge party for her in Lakewood, which we attended along with Elisha, Chad, and the kids; Jim's aunts, uncles, and cousins; and ladies from Lucille's parish. We placed a tiara on Lucille's head and she held court like a queen, greeting every guest, shaking hands and kissing cheeks. She basked in the attention, and I was grateful we had spent the time and money to pay tribute to this modest lady.

Shortly after, she developed dementia and gradually lost the ability to adequately care for herself so, at ninety-four, Lucille moved from an assisted living facility into a nursing home. Jim and I had traveled 3000 miles to help his brother with the final purging of garage, closets, cupboards, cubby holes, file cabinets, dresser drawers—and the shadowy recesses of the pantry—in the family home. Before we arrived, Paul rented a dumpster and had it deposited in the back yard. I never understood Joe, keeper of receipts, report cards, schoolbooks, church meeting minutes, mysterious chemicals, old cars, tools, batteries, lawn mowers, Christmas cards, and picture albums. The man I never got along with, the man from whom my husband fled some forty years ago, the man whose towering expectations no one, save maybe the Pope and Jesus, had ever met. The racist who hated the "damn free-loading Mexicans" next door as well as the "damn no-good Blacks" who slowly moved into his neighborhood. The man who could smile and say, "You look nice today," but it wasn't a compliment.

Jim and Paul (five years younger) grew up in the once-rural community of Lakewood, Colorado, on the outskirts of Denver. When the boys were young, the town still carried some of its farming heritage; houses were built on large lots where people could still grow personal crops and keep chickens, turkeys, horses, and donkeys. As Lakewood grew, so did the suburbs of Denver, encircling them during the nearly seventy years Jim's parents lived in the same house.

Joe had grown up on a farm in Nebraska, the oldest boy of eleven children in a German Catholic family. His parents spoke German and he grew up speaking that language as well as English. As the eldest boy, Joe was expected to become the family priest, the keeper of the family's spiritual well-being, their personal representative to God. At seventeen he was shipped off to seminary to begin the journey toward the priesthood, bowing to the wishes of his father, the man Joe's sons remembered as harsh and unforgiving, and with an explosive temper.

But while still in the seminary and serving at a Denver parish, Joe met Lucille, a petite, lively beauty with dark curls and a bright smile. Lucille had also come from rural Nebraska, moving to Denver with her two sisters to find work during World War II. Joe and Lucille fell in love. They struggled with their forbidden feelings. They confessed. They consulted the parish priest. Joe could fulfill his family's wishes, or he could follow his heart. Lucille left the decision to him. The church offered security, contemplation, ritual, and service. Earthly love promised unpredictability, intimacy, children, and hard choices. Joe chose Lucille.

After the war, Joe and Lucille purchased the house we were now excavating, a small brick home on a lot that had once been a chicken farm. It had a large outbuilding, once housing the chicken coops and since converted to a garage with enough storage to contain everything needed for a farm, though the land had long been reduced to smaller lots. Joe never really abandoned his farming roots or work ethic; even though he worked as a chemist for the county highway department, he took a second job selling Kraft foods to retailers to pay for his sons to attend Catholic school. He obtained permission from the county to plant an acre of corn and vegetables beneath the high-voltage power lines on their street, and used the water in the community irrigation ditch to cultivate his crops.

When raising his boys Joe adopted his father's harsh disciplinary style, and the same demands for work and conformity. Though Joe had little time for his boys, never attending their baseball or football games or other activities, he believed in education and the Church. He demanded the boys score high grades and adhere strictly to Catholic doctrine. He expected them to follow the same work ethic he displayed on his small farm, and to help with all of the chores needed on their house and property. Jim found his father's standards, demands for compliance, and constant criticism stifling and oppressive. Jim escaped this environment as soon as he left for college, and never returned.

***

From the tiny closet I retrieved a pair of short-sleeved zip-up coveralls, the kind of garb Joe wore everywhere except to church and his own funeral. Another cloud of decades' old dust erupted into the stuffy basement air. Next, a pair of gray striped bib overalls, legs dotted with tiny holes no doubt from some toxic liquid Joe brought home from his work with the highway department. Trash. "I can't do this," I said. "I'm choking up."

"I'm sorry," Jim said. "I didn't realize you and Dad were so close."

He got a half-hearted smile out of me. "My allergies."

Jim jerked a faded red plaid shirt from a rusty hanger and heaved it into the trash. "Go on. Get out of here. I'll finish."

Upstairs, sunlight filtered through the Virgin Mary, the prisms, the blue and red hummingbirds, the angels, and other baubles dangling from fishing line in the kitchen bay window, casting rainbows on the pictures, papers, and file folders stacked on the table. Though I breathed more easily here, I was overwhelmed at the canned food, dishes, silverware, mixers, bags of flour, and all manner of debris strewn on the countertops. In the living room, piles of clothing and linens covered a sofa, a tattered rocking chair, and a good portion of the hardwood floor. Jim's brother had been trying to clear the house for weeks but had so far made little progress. Now we were slowly organizing the objects into categories. Donations to charity. Recyclables: paper, glass, aluminum, and metal. Hazardous materials. Trash (everything left over.) I didn't see how we would ever clear the place out in five days.

I lifted a file folder from the top of one pile and a black-and-white photo slipped out. I picked it up. Men in wide-brimmed hats, crumpled jeans, shirts with rolled sleeves. Women in flowered housedresses, toddlers and babies in their arms. I recognized Jim as a child, wearing shorts but no shirt. He burrowed into his mother's skirt, his eyes seemingly asking, "Who are these people?" Joe's father stood in the center of the picture, hatless, his overalls stretched over a slight paunch. Joe's mother huddled among her grown children and grandchildren, her light-colored hair swept up, a wave drooping over her forehead. A full-length apron covered most of her printed dress. She looked weary, the kind of weary that comes from bearing and raising eleven children, working a farm, and trying to feed her family. Absent from the picture, Joe must have been the photographer. On the back, near the right-hand corner, inscribed in delicate script, he had captioned it, *End of threshing, August, 1953*. I opened the folder and found another photo with the same backdrop. Joe, Lucille, and Jim, still backed up into his mother's skirt, posed with Joe's parents. Joe's shirt looked spotless, his pants pressed, a city boy visiting, the only sibling who left their small Nebraska hometown.

I could not identify any of the other people in the rest of the photos in the folder, so set it aside. I picked up a bulging envelope crammed with more pictures and pulled one out. Two donkeys, the larger one nuzzling the ear of the pale fuzzy one beside her. Behind them, bare trees, scraped ground, a picket fence, a large half-barrel feeding trough. The neatly penciled script on the back of the photo reads *Daisy and Danny*. The scene was here, beside this house, near the old chicken coop, subsequent repository of old paint, pesticides, rusty nails, chain saws, and dead Volkswagens. No matter this city lot was bone dry, or the gigantic metal scaffolding of high voltage power lines towered over it. Joe let no piece of ground lay idle. Using the old irrigation ditch running alongside the house, he transformed the dusty soil into arable land, planting beets, potatoes, tomatoes, lettuce, peas, green beans, and asparagus. Sweet corn flourished. A crabapple tree produced tart red fruit for jelly, and grapevines hugged the filigree of the wrought iron carport. Between his two jobs, Joe spent time in the cornfield or in the garden or with the animals. A getaway cabin he bought to relax in the mountains turned into weekends of building, remodeling, and tree-planting expeditions. His two sons were unwillingly enlisted to help with the drudgery of Joe's many projects.

But the donkeys served no functional purpose. They carried no burdens, plowed no fields. They were simply Joe's pets and confidantes. "I'd rather spend time with these donkeys than people," Joe used to say. "Won't let you down." What kind of man lavishes his affection on animals but denies it to the people closest to him? I knew beneath Jim's anger at his dad's perfectionism and rigidity lay a sadness he rarely expressed. Where was the father who might have shown up for sports games, organized birthday parties, enjoyed a walk in the outdoors instead of plowing, planting, or repairing a cabin?

Beneath the stack of folders and envelopes crammed with photos lay a wooden jewelry box, mahogany-colored, beat-up and scratched. I lifted it, meaning to set it aside—just more of Lucille's costume jewelry. But clinking metal made me pause. Coins? Could be worth something. The tiny brass latch popped open easily. Inside, against a rich purple velvet lining, a muddle of red, blue, and gold military medals with embroidered insignias and brass pins. I shook the box to spread them out, picked them up one at a time, holding each in my hand, feeling their weight, admiring their color and shine. Then I remembered the trunk.

Not long after Joe died, while Lucille was still living here, I had helped Jim and Paul sort through boxes of Joe's belongings stored in a corner of the boys' old basement bedroom. Beneath several boxes we discovered a dented metal footlocker. Jim pried open the reluctant latch and cracked the weighty lid. Joe's army dress uniform lay neatly folded on top. Beneath were fatigues for everyday service. The material was faded, but still sharply creased. Nearer the bottom we found a smashed hat. Jim grabbed the bill, shook it, and the top popped up, revealing gold braids and German lettering.

Digging deeper, Jim extracted Nazi insignias, patches, brass buttons, another cap, and a Nazi uniform. I drew back, too repulsed to touch these macabre souvenirs. Where did they come from? Did Joe strip the bodies of Germans he had killed?

"What exactly did your dad do in the war?" I asked.

"Counterintelligence," Paul said. "He spoke German."

Joe? In counterintelligence? Maybe he wore the Nazi uniform and insignia. World War II spy movies flashed through my mind—American soldiers posing as Nazis behind enemy lines. But war hero did not fit my image of Joe. Cynical and contemptuous of all authority save the Church's and his own, he wasn't one to take risks, nor was he especially patriotic.

"Dad said he couldn't talk about what he did in the war," said Paul. "Sworn to secrecy."

"But there were those pictures," Jim said.

Rummaging through an old bookshelf when he was a young boy, Jim had one day discovered, between volumes of dusty books, an album he had never seen before. He opened the pages to sights not meant for little-boy eyes: stacks of naked corpses and living skeletons—men, women, and children dressed in rags. He flipped through page after page of horrifying scenes, trying to make sense of what he saw. When his dad came home, he took the book to him.

"What are these pictures?" Jim asked.

"They're not for you to see." Joe snatched the album without explanation, and the pictures vanished. Decades later, Jim learned Joe had taken the pictures himself at the liberation of the Bergen-Belsen concentration camp. But the rest of Joe's war history remained a mystery, locked away like the uniform in the trunk. What were the lasting effects on him of those sights, those horrors? Did he talk to anyone about them? Was any of his anger and hostility, his obsession with work some form of reaction to these experiences?

All of the fathers in my generation had fought in the war, but few talked about it. Most of what we knew about it came from movies glorifying the heroics of our side and demonizing the German and Japanese enemies, the war a distant past fought and won in faraway places. My father was a gunner in the Army Air Corps dropping bombs and shooting directly at enemy planes in missions flown over France and Italy. Crammed in a turret, where it was unbearably hot. "Sick the minute I got on the plane," he said. Vomiting while firing.

Back then, little was known about the lifelong effects of trauma and how to treat them. My father's plane was shot down but, like Joe and so many other men of their generation, he never shared with his family the horrors he had experienced.

Before we were done, we delivered seven carloads of clothing, linens, tools, furniture, garden supplies, books, and odds and ends to charity. We dumped a pantry-full of home-canned fruit and vegetables from Joe's garden—twenty, maybe thirty years old. We heaped a stout trailer with recyclable metals and filled the entire dumpster with junk that couldn't be given away or recycled. I packed a paper bag with folders and envelopes crammed with pictures and stuffed it in Jim's suitcase to carry home.

"I won't leave you a bunch of crap to sort through when I die," I promised my daughter when we got back home. Our own house now appeared cramped, cluttered, worn, and tired. Too many pictures, masks, and mementos on the wall; clothes, boots, and shoes I would never wear; books I would never read; notebooks full of old essays; papers from workshops; tax returns; CDs; journals filled with rambling scribbles. I was choking on the past, weighed down by the clutter around us. I wanted open space—blank space—to breathe. I didn't want Elisha to feel the burden of a broken-down inheritance like I did with the cabin on the lake or Jim did with his father's remnants.

On a rainy summer's day, I sat on the floor in the middle of my own sewing/guest/junk room, facing the detritus of my life. A recycle bin overflowed with papers and magazines. I was ruthless, even tossing out a stack of sentimental Mother's Day cards. In the corner behind a suitcase I spotted a bulging paper shopping bag we'd brought back from Colorado, a ragged picture album protruding from the top. I grabbed the bag by the handle and the whole thing ripped apart. Folders, loose pictures, and a purple notebook spilled out. Jim's childhood pictures scattered across the carpet—a kid on a trike, a toddler, a scowling teenager on a family road trip. The photos I recognized, but the spiral notebook was a mystery. We must have gathered it as we were leaving Joe and Lucille's house. I picked it up. Hand-lettering across the top read, *May 1990 thru 1997 Diary*. Inside the front cover was Joe's name, printed in thick black magic marker.

Joe—a diary?

I was curious, but hesitant. I was done with Joe. I had left him in Denver after completing the job no one wanted. We cleaned out the house which, after the brothers divided the estate, went to Paul, and I did not want to revisit those musty rooms.

I told Jim about my discovery that night at dinner. He wanted nothing to do with the diary. "Read it or toss it," he said. It didn't matter to him. I was angry all over again at Joe for never attempting to get close to his sons. His stained coveralls, his war medals, his pet donkeys were his legacies.

For several days I avoided the shabby notebook the way I had avoided Joe. It sat alone on the floor in the center of the room while I continued purging my past. I debated whether to dump it, shred it, or torch it in the wood stove, but I couldn't bring myself to get rid of it. Maybe he wanted someone to find it, but I had no right to it. To Joe, I was always an outsider. But then Jim felt like an outsider in his own family. He was the one who graduated from college, left home, left the church, got a divorce, married again. But Joe was gone now.

He couldn't hurt anyone.

Finally I opened the book and scanned the yellowed pages. Joe wrote in sloppy, short sentences, abbreviating words like he could not get them down fast enough. All of the entries were in May—eight years of Mays, no other months. A paragraph or two nearly every day in May, then a blank space before May Day of a new year.

I felt cheated, then puzzled. Why only May? I went back, reading the text slowly this time. It was a farmer's almanac of sorts, a record of daily weather and ritual. Morning mass (*Fr. Freeman is always late*). Weather report (*still sprinkling, with only 5/8 inch of rain*). Garden and yard work. Irrigation ditch repair. Dinner. Church meetings. Collapse in bed. Buried deep in the pages he declared May was his favorite month, the planting month. He tended his crops as if survival depended on them, but he seemed to derive little pleasure from his labor. Beneath his terse daily records, there was a sense of never doing enough, never having enough. He took joy only in his one grandchild, Selena, as she stalked mice in the cornfield, shopped for candy, read the lesson at Mass.

Increasingly his notations revealed a failing body. *I hurt so badly I stayed in bed most of the day, and inactive forenoon due to pain, and stiff and in pain—buttocks, hips, shoulders, hands . . . I'm real discouraged with life—can't work anything myself and there's so much to do.*

At age eighty, Joe wrote his final entry: *Beautiful May is gone . . . it's been a tough, painful one for the most part and I've done a poor job of keeping records.* Without the garden, without the energy to continue his routine, to keep moving, take care of his land, he was depressed, defeated. The work was too much for Lucille, and son Paul was too busy with his own life just trying to survive financially to spend the time taking care of his father's chores. In my mind, I fast forwarded my own life to when I might not be able to hike or bike or ski, or wander along a beach and gaze at birds, or even get out of bed, and I was flooded with a sense of loss—the loss of the body that has always responded to my will, always defined who I am. But more than that, I feared old age might inevitably bring regret—lost abilities, missed opportunities, and unfulfilled dreams. I wondered if Joe had any dreams. If so, did he share them with Lucille or anyone else?

To the end, Joe carried the burden of expectations unfulfilled—his father's that he become a priest, his sons' that he give them something more than constant work. He chose the messier path, through the horrors of war, the financial demands of a family, the turmoil of raising two boys, the struggle to fill his days with purpose.

One final, beautiful May came and went. In debilitating pain, Joe finally agreed to undergo back surgery. But when he got out of the hospital, the roof needed fixing. Against his doctor's orders, he climbed a ladder to the roof while Lucille was away. His back seized up and he could not climb down. Paul found him there on the roof, hours later, hoarse from yelling for help. He never quite recovered. In quick succession, there was emergency heart surgery, then pancreatic failure, and then he was gone.

I never said goodbye to Joe. I barely said hello. I resented him, avoided him. If I'd been less guarded, more curious, more courageous, I might have joined him in the garden, in May, his favorite month, when the soil was rich and damp, as a breeze rustled the bright new leaves. But I doubt it. Through his diary, I gained empathy for the pain he was going through, the same kind of back pain Jim was now suffering, for which he too would eventually require surgery. But thankfully, my husband has freed himself of Joe's emotional burden and can share his love with the people who also love him.

Chapter Seventeen

We couldn't find Neptune. After four hours I wanted to give up, but Jim was a shadow on the snowy trail ahead and he was not quitting. The setting sun: a pale orange stripe over the waters of Cook Inlet on a January day that never quite reached daylight. The temperature: somewhere near twenty degrees. The snow: like loose, grainy sand. I thought of Jack London's story, "To Build a Fire"; that's how my mind works, expect the worst and wait for it to happen. In London's tale an inexperienced man trying to complete an ordinary task commits a series of small but crucial missteps that lead him to the point of no return, which in the context of the far north's winter meant freezing to death. But today the temperature was not -75 degrees Fahrenheit, we were not in the Yukon, and we did not need to build a fire to survive. I also had emergency supplies in my backpack—energy bars, water, headlamps, chemical hand and toe warmers.

Jim's shadow disappeared. He was wandering off on his own again, now an unstoppable force hurtling away from us.

"We'll walk ten more minutes, and if we don't find Neptune we're turning around," I said to thirteen-year-old Cason for maybe the fourth time. What I was thinking was *We'll never find it. We started too late, delayed by Cason's hockey practice. It's not worth fifty science points. We should turn around.*

It started as a fun project, a chance to spend the day with our grandson. Now Cason and I trudged through the coarse snow in our heavy winter boots. Beside me, his red stocking cap nearly reached my cheek. Soon he would shoot past me. He was changing so fast I felt like I was meeting a new version of him each time we got together. Once his favorite subject was social studies, now he hated it. Once he was a snowboarder, now he only wanted to ski. Once he wanted to be a hunter, now he was happy to shoot at the range.

Lately, we mostly bickered.

"Quit treating me like a baby," he'd complain.

"Quit acting like one," I'd reply. I believed at his age he should be able feed the dog, wash his hands, set the table, or perform any of the tasks necessary to living in a household without debating me.

"Leave me alone," he'd say.

"Don't talk to me like that." I'd return.

In calmer moments, I understood he was only testing his power, wanting to grow up, make his own decisions. Other times I took deep breaths just to keep from screaming.

We walked together in semi-darkness, the lights of the nearby airport casting a faint pink glow on the dense cloud cover above us. The snow on the ground reflected the dim light upward, allowing us to perceive objects as silhouettes and shadows. In this diffuse light, I sensed a bond might still hold Cason and me together despite our squabbles, in spite of Cason growing up and me growing old.

When he had called the night before, I said yes, of course we'd help him with his science project. How often did he ask to spend time with us in his world of hockey, school, friends, video games, TV shows, and movies? He still needed us. Secretly—he would never admit such a thing—he must have thought we were smart, adventurous, and fit. Never mind that he had an entire two weeks of Christmas break to finish the project but had waited until the last day to get it done. His mom and dad said *no way* were they helping him, meaning we, the grandparents, were perhaps not brilliant, but gullible.

The mission: locate, photograph, and record data on all of the planets (and Pluto) stretched out in stations from the center of downtown Anchorage with its giant ceramic sun, to the end of the trail that runs alongside the treacherous mudflats of Cook Inlet, an earthly distance of a little over ten miles. This permanent installation, designed and written by a local high school student and crafted by local artists, is named the Anchorage Lightspeed Planet Walk. In the summer I had breezed by these brightly colored planetary stations on my bike, riding the ribbon of asphalt that snaked behind neighborhoods and along cliffs high above the glacial waters, cutting through old birch and cottonwood forest, skirting airport runways, then making a steep climb to connect with a vast network of skiing, biking, and hiking trails in Kincaid Park.

But it was winter now, and cold, and growing darker by the minute, so our plan had been to drive as close as we could to each planetary station, make our approach on foot (photographic evidence was required), then dash back to the car. In less than an hour, we had reached the Sun, Mercury, Venus,

Earth, and Mars. A quick drive and a short tromp to Jupiter. A brief stop to grab coffee, cookies, and cocoa before moving on to Saturn. To check off Uranus required a forty-five-minute jog, round trip. Another drive and we found Pluto, tucked beside a porta-potty next to Kincaid Park's ski chalet.

Only Neptune was left to find. According to the map at the first station downtown, it was an hour and fifteen-minute walk from Pluto. There were no GPS coordinates, nor landmarks provided. The sensible thing was to ask directions and, being the sensible one, I ventured into the ski chalet, where no one on the Parks and Rec staff could remember exactly where to find Neptune.

When I emerged, Jim and Cason had vanished. Unfortunately, Cason was learning the disappearing act from his grandfather. Fighting panic, I studied the three ski trails that diverged from the chalet. I could not trust my sense of direction; the little gyroscope in my brain is haywire, and simply finding my car in a parking lot can be a major undertaking.

I squinted in the faltering light. Ruts from fat-tired winter bikes. Footprints on top of ski tracks. The main multi-use trail the most likely, I followed it down the hill, walking briskly so I wouldn't second-guess myself. After ten minutes, then fifteen, there was still no sign of them.

I decided I'd better call Jim, but on the screen of my cell phone there was a big zero with a slash through it. No cell coverage. I walked ten minutes more, less briskly. Sweating, I unzipped my coat as I considered backtracking to the chalet. Damn them. The farther away from the ski chalet I traveled, the closer we moved toward the flight paths of the jets taking off and landing. A far cry from the small airport where my family landed in 1954, the Ted Stevens International Airport is now the fourth busiest airport in the world for cargo. Occasionally, one of the colossal cargo planes heading to or from Asia blasted over my head, requiring me to quickly cover my ears.

A couple advanced in my direction, holding hands. This was how it should be. People who love each other should stick together on the trail. Especially in winter.

"Have you passed a man and a boy?" A foolishly generic question, but the woman pointed, and there they were, just rounding a gentle curve in the trail, two dark figures against the snow, the skinny one almost as tall as the heavier one. I hurried to catch them.

Reunited, I resisted venting my fury. We still had to find Neptune.

Almost immediately, Jim surged ahead again. This is how it goes between us. Before cell phones, we carried walkie-talkies so I could let him know if a bear had attacked me and he could let me know—by his silence? by an uncharacteristic scream?—if he'd fallen over a cliff.

Cason, growing tired, stayed back with me, all of us, hopefully, hunting down Neptune. A skier approached—perfect glide, weight shifting from side to side, no wasted energy. If we had skied the solar system we would have been done already. But Cason the sprinter, the hockey player, the downhill skier, never took to cross-country skiing—too much trouble, he said. I interrupted the skier's stride to ask if he had seen Neptune, then explained in response to his stare that we were doing the planet walk and Neptune was our last planet. He informed us that if it was where he thought it was, we had another mile or so left. He also noted the obvious: it's already past sunset. As in, *Are you nuts?*

"We have headlamps," I informed him. He shook his head, then pushed off.

The cloud cover must have lifted slightly because our meager reflected light was dissolving. I left the headlamps in my pack, though, because I didn't want the single bright beam to reduce our eyes' sensitivity to objects beside the trail—moose or Neptune.

We trudged another ten minutes, then another ten. Cason announced he was hungry, his lunch of potato chips and Gatorade long gone from his backpack. He ripped open the energy bar I offered, then slowly jawed the cold, stiff mass of peanut butter and chocolate and swigged from my water bottle to wash it down. I too needed a boost, a cup of coffee or a piece of chocolate from my now-empty snack supply.

"Look!" said Cason.

Up ahead we could just discern two figures on the trail. Closer, Jim's unmistakable compact figure stood next to a skier. We watched him high-five the skier, do a little hop, and move a few steps up the trail. He saw us, but it was as if we had never been apart. His mind doesn't go where mine does, toward disasters arising from a series of missteps, the first of which is to separate from the group. He jabbed at the darkness beside the trail, and we knew he had found it: Neptune.

A hand-bump with Cason, and we were up the trail to join Jim at the big, opaque sphere protruding from a blue sign with white lettering. Blurred in the faint light, there's the old god of the sea with his scepter, a photograph of Neptune taken by Voyager 2, a representation of Neptune's moon, Triton, and a whole panel of facts. Though this is a sizable landmark on a pedestal reaching above our heads, it would be easy to pass by if you were on a bike, or skiing, or jogging, or even strolling, eyes on the trail, heading for your goal ahead, scanning for animals, thinking of your destination and dinner.

Cason snapped a picture with his cell phone, positioning it at a slant so the flash wouldn't create a glare on the metal display. Then he handed me the phone to document his discovery.

I was elated but also exhausted. Worry does this, and wanting: for all of us to stick together, for us to prove ourselves cool grandparents, for us to avoid the little wrong turns that would send us hurtling toward disaster. The exhaustion was also physical. We'd hiked three miles since Pluto, plus three miles earlier, and now it was three miles back to the car.

Cason wanted to rest. I tried to brush snow from a bench on the side of the trail, but it was coated with several inches of ice. The three of us plopped down anyway. My legs tingled. My neck ached. Below, in the black waters of Cook Inlet, gray chunks of ice floated past, moving in and out with the tides as they always do, whether we're watching or not.

"My butt's getting cold." Cason, then Jim stood. With three layers of clothing between the icy bench and me I would have liked to have lingered, but I followed them, elated and exhausted, following the trail to the long, winding hill leading to the warm chalet, a bathroom, our car, dinner. Cason's mom had promised us tacos. We'd promised Cason a stop at the ice cream shop.

At mid-trudge uphill Cason paused at a foot path veering from the trail through the snow toward a dark ridge. "Look," he said. "A short cut."

"I'm not so sure," I said.

Jim agreed with Cason that from here it did look like the path would cut some distance off this snaky trail up the hill. But I had hiked these side trails in the summer and they were a labyrinth of twists and turns and cross trails.

Cason started up the foot path. "I don't know if that path goes straight to the top. Those trails are confusing . . . we should stick together," I said.

The disaster wheel churned in my brain. There were too many trails at the top of the ridge. Cason would get confused. A moose might charge, hooves trampling him into the snow where he would lie alone, staring into the dark night, the whirling planets, until overcome by cold.

He lapsed into his thirteen-year-old stubborn self, turned his back to me, and hurried up the dark trail. I expected Jim to follow him along the shortcut, but instead he trudged ahead on our current route, in something of a trance, eyes straight ahead, one foot after the other up the sharp incline. Old snow boots and twisting steps in sloppy snow were not kind to his aging knees.

"He'll figure it out," said Jim, without looking back.

I was tired. Maybe I was more like my mother than I wanted to believe. Overprotective, predicting failure, holding her kids back from taking risks and making their own mistakes. Cason was growing up, whether I watched him or not. I would not be able to follow after him forever.

I let him go and stuck to the main trail. Fifteen, maybe twenty minutes passed. My cell phone rang. A few garbled words and Cason cut out. I called him back, frantic, but my call wouldn't go through. The phone rang again. "Mema," is all that came out before the line went dead.

This was, quite literally, my recurring nightmare: punching numbers into a phone, trying to connect with a person who needs me (or do I need him?) and the call never going through.

The phone rang again.

"Backtrack to the main trail if you're lost!" I hollered into the phone. The screen gave me the circle with the line through it again. I held the image of my grandson, warm and smiling, against my fear of him lying beaten and broken in the cold.

Another half hour and we reached the chalet, but no Cason. I dashed around the building, holding up my cell phone, trying to get a signal. Jim disappeared again, perhaps into the building, perhaps around to the ski trails on the other side; I didn't know. I was alone at the end of the solar system. Pluto—the demoted dwarf planet—hovered outside the door. I paced back and forth through a steady stream of hikers and skiers entering and leaving the warm building.

Finally, in the lights of the chalet, I spotted a bright red Detroit Red Wings stocking cap popping over the hill. I waved frantically and rushed over.

"I was so worried about you. What happened?"

"I couldn't figure out which trail, so I walked all the way down and came back on the main trail," he said, out of breath.

So he took my advice. Or maybe he never heard it. None of that mattered now.

"Smart thinking," I said. I teared up with relief and wanted to crush him with a hug, but settled for lightly touching his arm, a brush boding disaster for planets, separate in their orbits, but which for us meant simply *yes, I'm with you, we made it.*

That same winter, after our search for Neptune, I spent the night with the grandkids while their mom was away on a business trip and their dad worked his all-night at the fire station. Elisha sells and leases commercial real estate property in

Alaska and other western states. Her work sometimes takes her out of state to meet with clients or to her company's home office in Salt Lake City.

Since the kids no longer needed or wanted me to tell bedtime stories or tuck them in, I saw my role as basically chaperon and enforcer. They saw me as their driver and an unnecessary obstacle to their complete independence. It was true—they were mostly self-sufficient, Cason thirteen and Carly eleven. Cason juggled hockey before and after school and on weekends, earned straight As in middle school, fixed his own lunch, and got to the bus stop on time in the morning.

While I took his sister to figure skating practice, Cason microwaved Top Ramen for dinner and did his homework. He was watching a movie in his room when we got home. He wanted to be left alone, but I made him join us at the table while Carly and I ate, believing families should at least sit down together at dinnertime and say something to each other.

"How was your day?" I asked him.

Silence.

"What team are you guys playing this weekend?"

More silence. I gave up and excused him from the table. Carly and I continued eating and chatting about our respective days.

Later, the kids were upstairs in the final stages of getting ready for bed. Dolly, the fuzzy white dog, trotted up to join them while I relished a rare moment of tranquility in my daughter's house. I switched on the reading lamp, snuggled into the cushions of her soft leather sofa, tucked a fuzzy orange blanket around my legs, and opened my book. I marveled at the daily logistics of this family. My life as the parent of an only child was lonelier and poorer, but also simpler.

The jangle of my cell phone interrupted my brief reverie. On the other end, Elisha was sobbing.

"Rob killed himself today,"

Their good friend Rob. The man I spoke with at the ice rink while Carly and his daughter were taking lessons. Father of Cason's hockey pal.

The fun dad.

The camping and dirt-biking dad.

The church-going, homework-helping, hard-working, successful dad.

This morning, while his kids and wife were away from the house, he aimed a gun at his head and fired. He left no note. He gave no warning, at least none any of us recognized.

"I am so, so sorry," I said. Sorry for Rob's family and ours, and for all the pain rippling out from a single desperate decision. For the lifelong trauma of losing a husband and a father to suicide and the guilt that inevitably follows, for the financial crisis created with the loss of a major breadwinner, for the unraveling of lives and dreams once woven so closely together.

"Do you want me to tell the kids?" I asked Elisha.

In the world of texts and Instagram there would be no secrets. If someone didn't tell them now, they would read the news on their cell phones instantly.

"Give Chad a few minutes," she was still sobbing. "He'll call from the fire station and tell them. Could you just help out after they talk?"

"Sure," I said. Chad's a good dad. He would know what to say. I just had to be there for them. I wanted to be close to the kids, to be the kind of grandma they could talk to, the kind who was not afraid to answer hard questions. But now I was a coward. I couldn't explain the unexplainable. In their lives, death is for old people. Just days ago, they had spent the weekend with Rob and his family at Elisha's cabin, tubing, biking, and soaking in the hot tub together.

I sat still for several seconds, heart thumping, stomach grinding. If only I had some sort of religion to fall back on. The faith I abandoned in my twenties would have come in handy now. *Rob's in a better place. He's at peace.* None of that made any sense, though. A man who seemed to have everything loses all hope. It made me wonder whether we ever really know anyone.

One cell phone rang upstairs, then not long after, the other. I waited a few minutes, frozen in place, then headed up to the kids' bedrooms. Dolly greeted me at the top of the stairs. She jumped on my shins, scratched my legs, then whirled and darted between Cason and Carly, who stood at opposite ends of the hallway.

Carly was nearest, in the doorway of her parents' bedroom, in her robe with a towel wrapped around her head.

"Dad told you about Rob?" I said, knowing he had.

"I have lots of questions," she says. "But Dad says no one knows the answers yet. Mom's going to call later."

She ducked into her bedroom and shut the door.

A few steps away, in his bedroom doorway, her brother began to weep, a torrent of grief. I hesitated. Abandoning his no-hugging rule, I crossed the distance between us and drew his body close to mine. He rested his head on my shoulder as I stroked his spiky hair.

"Why would Rob do that?" he sobbed.

"Sometimes people hurt so badly inside they can't see any other way to stop the pain," I said.

"How do they know it wasn't murder?" he asked.

There were so many ways to know I didn't want to tell him. Instead, I talked about depression, about how people might seem okay on the outside, but something is wrong inside their brains, and they need medicine and other people to help them.

He wanted to know why Rob didn't get help. Or if he tried to get help but it didn't work.

"I don't know," was all I could say. "I'm sure he loved his family," I said. "I'm sure he didn't mean to hurt them."

I didn't know what else to say. There were no good answers. I tried hard not to be judgmental, but I was angry even though I barely knew the man.

"Your parents love you very much," I said. "They would never do anything like this."

Cason lay down on his bed. I gathered the dog into my arms and sat down on the bed next to him, placing the dog between us. We stroked her soft fur and talked about Rob's family, his wife and two kids, and how everyone needed to help them out now. How they would need help for a long time.

Finally, Cason said he was ready to go to sleep. "Leave the door open," he said.

"I love you," I said.

I opened Carly's bedroom door and peeked in on her. She lay in bed, covers pulled up to her chin, headphones plugged into her ears, her face bathed in the blue glow of her cell phone.

"Are you okay?" I asked. Walked to her side, leaned over and kissed her cheek.

She nodded her head without looking up and waved me away. I walked back down the stairs to the guest room.

While I brushed my teeth in the downstairs bathroom, Cason appeared at the door.

"Mema," he said, "Could I watch a funny show I recorded on my iPad? I wanna stop thinking about all this."

"Sure," I said.

"Thanks." He hesitated. "I love you."

If there hadn't been a gun in the house.

If his wife had gotten home earlier.

If the days were not slipping into fall.

If some chemical had been present or absent in Rob's brain.

If he had taken a deep breath and thought about the effects of this one action.

But none of that happened. He pulled the trigger. Ended his life. Destroyed the illusion of a safe and predictable world.

Long before the sun slipped above the snow-covered mountains to the east, I swallowed my first sip of coffee. Head aching, brain foggy, sinuses throbbing, I felt like I had stayed up all night drinking. After sending the dog out into the frosty back yard, I climbed the stairs to see if Cason was awake. His school started earlier than Carly's.

"Time to get up." I tugged gently at his toes. He moaned.

Downstairs the dog scratched at the sliding door to come back in. I shook a half-cup of dry food into her bowl, then let her in.

As I washed out my coffee cup, Cason appeared in the kitchen. He scavenged in the fridge, then in the cupboard, looking for possible lunch items. Potato chips and a peanut butter sandwich slipped into Ziploc bags. Ice in his water bottle. His lunch was packed. I started fixing his usual breakfast. Just half, he tells me. I handed him a lightly toasted cheese bagel smothered in butter.

"Anytime you want to talk more about last night . . ." I said.

"Yeah." A pause. "I will."

He grabbed a jacket. Before heading out the door to the bus stop, he wrapped an arm around my waist and hugged me. I brushed the top of his ball cap with a kiss.

Chapter Eighteen

One morning in early July, my friend Kathy and I left our sleeping husbands at a cabin in Homer, Alaska and headed for one of our favorite trails. Back in Alaska for a summer visit, Kathy was my hiking buddy, my birding friend, my coffee partner. Two years ago, she had ended a thirty-year love affair with Alaska and moved with her partner to Colorado for shorter winters and proximity to family. I missed her companionship and cherished this time alone with her, doing what we both love—rambling along a trail—before she left again. No mountains to scale, no rivers to ford, no great physical challenges this morning, just a path through spruce forest, over streams and across meadows, marsh, and wetlands. We planned to scout for bog wildflowers and try to identify songbirds by their calls.

We had heard from a local birding friend there were Northern Goshawks nesting near the trail. I had seen goshawks from a distance, but never close up. They are stealthy gray-and-white hunters with a distinctive white stripe over their red-orange eyes and, with broad wings and long tails acting as rudders, they are agile flyers. I wondered what their nest looked like, whether it would be as big as an eagle's. Also, this late in summer there would likely be chicks. This could be my chance for a picture of chicks in the nest.

It was also my chance to show Kathy her first goshawk. She was a beginning birder, the kind who does not yet wear a pair of binoculars like a necklace all summer, the way I do. I've been hooked on chasing birds since my first Kachemak Bay Shorebird Festival here in Homer more than thirty years ago. Kathy looked to me as the expert. "What's that bird?" she'd ask, pointing to a faraway blur, or hearing a trill somewhere in the trees. I did my best to be accurate—trying to find the bird with my binoculars, checking my bird app, comparing screen shots, playing recorded calls—but I had yet to reach the precision of the pros at the local Audubon Society, with their keen eyes and ears.

A night of heavy rain had turned the empty parking lot at the trailhead into brown soupy puddles. Though the rain had stopped not long ago and the sun now filtered through a weak layer of clouds, we donned rain pants, jackets, rubber boots, and rain hats to protect us from the wet grass and boggy path.

We began on high ground in a stand of mature spruce—a fairytale copse dense enough to block the rain and smelling of pitch, needles, and fungus. The ground sprang beneath our feet, softened by thick layers of spruce needles and the outer shells of spruce cones picked apart by generations of industrious squirrels. At a footbridge spanning a clear brook, we lingered in the soft light beneath the trees, admiring a patch of yellow monkey flowers, a kind of wild snapdragon thriving along the edges of streams.

The trail entered the bright light of a meadow, lush with chest-high grass and cow parsnip, a tall, celery-like stalk with flat, dinner-plate-sized leaves. As we stepped out of the trees, we heard a loud *kak kak* from the edge of the clearing. My first thought was a yellowlegs, a large sandpiper that nests in marshes. But the call was much too loud.

Kak kak kak kak. A gray streak hurtled toward us, inches above the grass, heading straight between our heads. Goshawk!

We dropped, knees to the muck, arms crossed, shielding our eyes. "My god!" I said. "Out of nowhere!"

"It almost hit me," said Kathy.

We struggled off the ground, stumbling in our awkward boots. Out in the open we were easy targets. We couldn't turn back—the bird had flown in that direction. If we could just get across the field . . .

Kak kak kak.

I froze as the distant shape shot toward us, becoming eyes, beak, and talons. I marveled at its outstretched wings, unflapping, tilting slightly side to side, correcting course. Aiming straight for me. Straight for my eyes.

We dove. A breeze from the bird's wings glanced across my cheek. I gasped and tried to flatten my body into the weeds, arms wrapped over my scalp, but we were hard targets to miss. Mouth dry, tongue thick, sweat dripping down the inside of my shirt, I whispered to Kathy, "How will we make it across this field?"

"Got to get to the other side," she said. Crouching as low as our cranky knees would allow, we stumbled across the field, boots sucking in the mud, rain pants swishing as they flapped against our legs. Reaching a clutch of ragged black spruce, we huddled beneath their thin branches, cowering from a bird a tenth our size. The scene from Alfred Hitchcock's movie *The Birds* flashed back to me. A flock of crows gathered in a schoolyard and, when the children left the building, the birds attacked them, trying to rip open their scalps and poke out their eyes.

This hawk definitely had murder on its mind. Even here, under the trees, we might not be safe. With their broad tails and wide wing spans, goshawks are masters of maneuvering among trees. Kathy rotated her fanny pack and water bottle back into place. With trembling hands, I adjusted my twisted binoculars straps and straightened the brim of my hat. I had been dive-bombed by Arctic terns protecting their nests, but those were false charges, the terns never coming closer than a foot from my head.

"No one will believe this," I said.

"The guys will think we're exaggerating," said Kathy.

Minutes passed. A story came back to me suddenly, one I'd forgotten until that moment. A friend, on a kayaking trip to a remote Alaskan island, told of coming ashore, hauling her gear along the trail to a rented Forest Service cabin, and being dive-bombed by a bird that ripped the hat from her head. A goshawk. Not so surprising, then, that Attila the Hun carried the image of a Northern Goshawk on his helmet.

With my binoculars, I searched the clearing behind us. No sign of the bird. A varied thrush whistled in the distance. All else was silent. We could have retreated, but would have risked getting strafed again. Plus, we had looked forward to this hike, saving it until the end of Kathy's trip, and neither one of us liked to back down on a goal once we had made up our minds.

"I'm not turning around," Kathy said.

"Me neither."

"Maybe it will be hunting when we come back."

"Or feeding the chicks in the nest," I said, but then I remembered both goshawk parents tend the chicks, one hunting while the other stays at the nest. And we had no idea exactly where the nest was.

We continued over roots, through puddles, around alders until we came upon a squirrel lying in the middle of the path, on its side, legs stretched out, eye unblinking. It looked intact. No sign of injury. When I nudged it with my foot, it flinched and blinked. It was either paralyzed or stunned.

"The goshawk?" Kathy offered.

I envisioned the squirrel in freefall, dropped for later while the bird took on human intruders, chilling evidence of the hawk's lethal ferocity. The goshawk had such a ruthless reputation for killing rodents and other birds, an early ornithologist, George Miksch Sutton, referred to it as "thoroughly undesirable" and "a savage destroyer of small game and poultry." In fact, its name comes from the old English "goose hawk" after its ability to capture and devour avian prey.

"Thank God we're not squirrels," I said.

We reached a wooden walkway winding through the boggiest part of the trail, safe under the cover of old spruce and dense alders, to our destination, a viewing platform overlooking Beluga Lake and a vast surrounding wetland. Here was prime habitat for swans, ducks, shorebirds, osprey, northern harriers, and moose, as well as bog wildflowers.

I scanned the marsh with my binoculars and spotted a moose, head and shoulders poking above the grass. On hearing our voices he raised his head, revealing an immense rack of antlers. He decided we were too far away to bother him, so lowered his head again and continued grazing.

We took our time at the lake, discussing Kathy's new hiking group in Colorado, dallying to examine the ripening cloudberries growing on single stems in the dark saturated soil, admiring the just-opening claret-colored marsh cinquefoils, and taking turns scouring the treetops with my binoculars for the white-crowned sparrow calling nearby.

We were procrastinating. Reaching our destination was not as sweet as we'd hoped, knowing we might get slashed by the knife-like talons of an enraged hawk on our way back. Our options were few—returning the way we had come, detouring through marshy water over our boots, or following a side trail we had never taken, one we believed came out a long way from the car.

Finally, the mosquitoes feasting on our ears and necks forced us to move. Examining the depth of the water in the bog beside us, we ruled out the swamp detour, so we faced back the way we had come, climbing over slippery roots in the cover of the forest, raingear drenched from the wet brush and dampened with sweat at the prospect of another attack. I unzipped my jacket but left it on for protection. My heart thump-thumped against the binoculars bouncing on my chest. I tightened the chin strap on my thin rain hat, its broad black brim with red center a perfect bull's eye from above.

We reached the fork connecting to the side trail. I knew it eventually wound up at the local elementary school, but didn't know how far it would take us out of our way or what condition that part of the trail was in after all the rain. And we'd have to walk back along the paved road, then down a neighborhood street and finally to the parking lot and trail head. We debated. Maybe the goshawk had picked the squirrel up and gone back to its mate on the nest. Maybe there were other people on the trail by now and they were the ones getting strafed. Maybe the goshawk was busy tearing the squirrel apart for the chicks. We were in denial. We chose the known hazard over the unknown terrain.

We reached the edge of the meadow. Silence. The coast seemed clear. We dashed a few steps.

Kak kak kak.

The gray bullet streaked toward us. Now we were squirrels running for our lives. The hawk swooped low. "Drop! Drop!" We crumpled to the earth as a feathered wind blasted over our heads. We struggled up and stumbled a few steps before the bird rocketed back for us. We slammed back down to the ground, shins plastered in the soft mud, arms wrapped over our heads. It was the duck-and-cover move we had learned in elementary school—but without the cover. We made a break for it. Bent at the waist, we two grandmothers in heavy gear sprinted for the safety of the spruce grove as if our lives depended on it. We reached the parking lot streaked with mud and dripping with sweat, but intact.

My hands trembled as I fumbled in my pack for the car keys. "It aimed right for my eyes."

"I thought it would rip off my scalp," said Kathy.

A narrow escape. Yet I admired the goshawk's fierce protection of its young, the kind I could have used from my young, overwhelmed parents during our early years in Alaska. And its restraint, to which I was a testimony, still having my eyes and my scalp. I longed for the kind of wisdom signaling when to attack and when to hold back in defense of the ones I love.

The next day an article in the Homer Tribune reported that our trail had been closed. *Posted: Keep out. Nesting goshawks. Attacks have occurred.*

Chapter Nineteen

It was March. A decade had passed since Mom died. Another decade since we'd built the new cabin at Nancy Lake. Heavy snows had fallen over the past two months, then came a windstorm and melting Chinook, followed by another foot of snow last week. The cabin, seldom used anymore and no longer so new, might have been crushed by trees, or collapsed with snow, or ripped apart by thieves. No one had visited since before Christmas, so my sisters asked me to check on it. I agreed to stop by, dreading what I might find, resenting I was still not completely free of the place.

With Elisha and her family having their own cabin now, and with no need for two cabins, she had signed over the share of the family cabin I had given her to my sisters. It belonged solely to Patty and Teri now. On this weekend, Jim and I were staying at Elisha's cabin, enjoying time with the grandkids playing Yahtzee, assembling puzzles, skiing on the frozen lake, and soaking in their outdoor hot tub.

No one had been plowing the long driveway to Teri's and Patty's cabin all winter, so there was no way to access it from the road. So one morning, before the kids were up, I snapped into my cross-country skis and headed across the frozen lake into a piercing north wind. Thin clouds veiled a pallid sun. My nose dribbled and my eyes watered beneath my goggles. I paused to retrieve the hood from the little pocket at the back of my nylon ski jacket and tied it securely under my neck, a slight improvement. I slipped into a snowmobile track, found my glide, and picked up speed, aiming for the small cove where the family cabin stood. Past a new stone house, as big as a lodge. Past a one-room turquoise hut with a bent stove pipe. Past a cedar home with white lights strung on posts around an ice rink lost in snow. I should have been there by now, but nothing looked right. Landmarks were buried in deep snow; colossal residences with their boat sheds, lifts, and docks had replaced small one-room structures; some lots had been completed cleared of trees. This was not the terrain I remembered.

I spotted a pitched gray roof on four naked posts. Was that the neighbor's fire pit where they would sit beside their bonfires even in the rain and drink all night? I glanced to the opposite shore, looking for the old marina where people used to rent canoes and paddleboats. But it had been gone for years. Nothing but modern homes sprawled along the opposite shore.

I reached the shoreline where snowmobile trails converged on a frozen swamp studded with black spruce. How could I have missed it? Had my memory become so frayed I couldn't even locate my parents' property? Confused, I retreated, veering off into deep snow, seeking signs of anything familiar. Face burning from the wind yet sweating from the effort of plowing through the snow, I unzipped my jacket and opened my chest to the cold. *Damn my lousy sense of direction. I can't go back to town and admit to my sisters I couldn't find the cabin!*

I turned around, then slid back to my own tracks. I passed the same tall gray roof perched above clean, untrammeled snow. It looked different from this side. The skeleton of an empty boat lift. The slight hump of a dock. I skied closer. Near the snow-covered dock I saw it, finally: the dark shape of the cabin, tucked deep in the snow, farther from shore than I remembered. I herringboned up a slight hill to get a closer look, my skis slicing the crusty knee-deep snow. A hodgepodge of chairs, a small table, a citronella candle, and assorted junk lay scattered on the front porch beneath the eaves. The place looked small, shabby, and abandoned. What was left of my parents' prized piece of Alaska—a lonely little shack. A surge of grief and anger swept through me. All the work to rebuild the cabin, the family togetherness, the hopes of leaving this to our children, gone. In all my years of hating the place, I still believed in the *idea* of the cabin as my parents' modest legacy. Now it seemed no one wanted it. My sisters did not have the time, money, or energy to maintain the cabin adequately, or the commitment to visit it, yet they refused to sell it. They scraped enough money together to share the costs of electricity, taxes, and insurance, but could have better spent the money on essentials in their everyday lives. Teri was especially tied to it since she had spent much of her teenage years having fun there, and she wanted to leave it to her son. Neither of them was ready to part with it yet.

I swiped a mitten across my nose and shivered. Time to move. I worked my way around the cabin. The porch and roof appeared intact. No broken windows. But the back stairs sagged and twisted away from the porch. The long narrow driveway, layered with several feet of snow, was a jumble of bent and fallen spruce, willows, and alders. Only a crew with chainsaws and muscles could clear that mess.

I side-stepped to the front steps, unclipped my skis, and stepped carefully onto thick slabs of ice, the fall line from the steeply pitched metal roof. I peered in the window but could see little around the drooping blue curtains. The key, hidden in the old real estate lock box, installed to allow multiple family members with the code to stop by and use the cabin, did not give itself up willingly in the cold. I tried the little knobs until my finger ached. Now that I was there, I wanted in. I wanted to remember what was inside—the pictures, the furniture, the trinkets left over from the old cabin. Pieces of our family's life.

I leaned down and squinted at the little box. I could make out the engraved numbers more easily from this angle, and when I entered the code again, the lever moved and the key dropped down.

Inside the air was cold and stale, as if winter were trapped there and couldn't escape. Grimy mattress pads lay stacked in corners. The expensive oil stove was unplugged; my sisters had told me it was no longer working. The refrigerator door was propped open, empty, save for two boxes of baking soda.

I climbed the stairs to the loft. Beds without linens. More sleeping pads stacked against the railing. A musty smell. Even the paint looked scuffed and dirty.

Back on the main floor, I switched on the light—still working. On the wall, the picture of Dad standing on the porch of the old cabin, smiling in his captain's hat with the gold braiding. Beside it, the faded picture Jim took so long ago of a ptarmigan transforming from winter white to spring brown plumage, and nearby, a picture I'd forgotten—an alpine lake, as blue-green as a turquoise pendant, lying at the base of a bowl-shaped valley. Dad took that photo while sheep hunting when he was young and new to Alaska. He had never climbed a mountain, never hunted, never made his way in wild terrain. I remember the story well—he had told it many times—his long labor up the slope, spotting the ram, shooting the strong and beautiful animal, the long journey down the mountain to bring the meat back to his family. Yet, it was not the ram's picture he hung on our wall. It was the jewel of a lake, viewed from a height reached with grit and determination, not taken with the skill and practiced eye of Jim's ptarmigan, but an indelible moment in the discovery of this new terrain.

This was the father I carried with me, the man who, before his drinking and the health problems, paused to capture a moment of beauty in his journey up a mountain, the man who turned me loose in the woods, the reason I would never settle for a boggy patch of land like this.

I turned to leave, and as I locked the door and fumbled with the cranky lock once more, I glanced up at the debris-clogged driveway. The swamp was winning. Again.

Let it win. Let the alders grow. Let the cabin sink, the outhouse rot, the lily pads creep over the dock, the muskrats nest beneath its floating planks, the floods lap against the cabin steps, the blueberries reclaim the shoreline. Let the whole place turn into a midden for future generations to ponder. Mom and Dad had joined the detritus on the bottom of the lake. Their legacy was not this place. We were their legacy.

I clipped my boots back into my skis, pushed off, and glided quickly down the gentle slope to the lake. I followed my own tracks back to my daughter's cabin. It was a place for their speedboat and four-wheelers and dirt bikes, a place for friends and kids to gather. Not my kind of place, but a place where I could visit, play with the kids, help with projects, ski across the lake. A place without ghosts or expectations.

As I skied around three perfectly round windows augured into the frozen lake by some winter angler, I took in the quiet. I felt lighter, the old place behind me, the new place, full of life and clatter and hope, ahead. In between, I was alone on the ice. Free.

Chapter Twenty

There were easier ways to celebrate thirty years of marriage, but I wanted to see the bears. The fat fishing bears at Brooks Falls in Alaska's Katmai National Park.

We could have hired a bush flight to dash us across the waters of Cook Inlet for a few hours of bear watching from a safe distance, fill a memory card with pictures, then fly back to the city to toast champagne over a fancy dinner. Mission accomplished. But we chose the hard way, on water, where we began our love affair on a raging river with a leaky raft. Thirty years of these waterborne adventures had brought us closer together, split us apart, even nearly killed us. Rivers, lakes, oceans. Raft, dory, kayak, canoe. Talachulitna, Alsek, Kongakut, Nigu, Canning, Colorado.

My husband Jim had seen plenty of bears, having worked for a year on Kodiak Island, the home of the largest bears in North America. But I hadn't. At least not like this. This time, as with our first trip, we chose the wrong vessel, the wrong time of year, the wrong itinerary. Eighty miles of paddling—

across the vast Lake Grosvenor, down the Savonoski River, and across the Iliuk Arm of Naknek Lake, a long, hard water route—culminating in a great gathering of bears at Brooks River in Katmai National Park.

From late June through early September as many as fifty brown bears at a time convene at Brooks Falls to fish for salmon migrating upstream to spawn. The fish must leap over the falls to get to their spawning grounds, making them easy targets for bears standing in and along the river. Since the installation of a webcam trained on the bears' favorite fishing spot twenty-four hours a day (the "Brooks Falls Bearcam"), the bears have achieved international fame. Peak bear viewing months are July, when the salmon are heading up Brooks River to spawn, and September, when most have spawned out and the dead and dying fish provide plentiful food for the bears needing to store fat for the long winter. People from all over the world who would never visit Katmai follow the bears on social media, giving them names, participating in chat groups, commenting on the bears' appearances. The park even conducts a fat bear contest every season in which people vote for the bear they think the most massive.

We were camped on the shore of Lake Grosvenor on the second day of an eight-day guided trip to Brooks Falls. I lay awake in our tent, staring out the small plastic window at our feet. I saw nothing but the gray swells and the white foam of waves on the lake, as if we were adrift on the ocean, yet our white and yellow dome tent was tethered securely by stout metal poles and brightly-colored ropes against the pummeling wind. Jim lay on his inflatable mattress next to me, asleep, eyes covered with a blue bandana to blot out the bright twilight of this late August evening. He was as oblivious to my distress as when he had wandered away from our camp on Kachemak Bay, or when we had left Elisha on the rock to climb Kesugi Ridge, or any of the other times he wandered away, physically or mentally focused on his own internal journey.

I tossed and turned and got tangled in my sleeping bag.

"This was your idea," I said.

"No, it was yours." He said, eyes still covered.

"We could have gone to Paris."

"You could have backed out."

I didn't tell him how many times I almost did. Our last canoe trip was decades ago, across a series of placid lakes with a few portages. Though we had practiced paddling across Nancy Lake in preparation for the trip, I feared my arms might not be strong enough for a multi-day trip. His shoulder, never the same after his bike accident and surgery, might give out. And the wind—in this part of Alaska—was the bane of water travel.

I fretted over all these concerns, even sharing some of them with Jim. But we had committed to exploring new terrain in Alaska every summer as long as our bodies would carry us. We were determined not to abandon wilderness travel as had some of our friends, proclaiming they were too old to continue.

"Are you sure you want to do this?" Jim asked me that spring when the final payment for the trip was due.

"Sure," I said, too stubborn to admit my misgivings.

Nothing about this wave-pummeled beach camp—nor our frantic thrashing to reach it—resembled the serene paddling of our practice on Nancy Lake or of our honeymoon at the unfinished cabin on Kachemak Bay. Day by day, I was reminded of why this trek was an unwise idea.

After arriving in the fishing village of King Salmon by jet, we were grounded there for most of the day by wind, low ceiling, and rain, waiting for the floatplane to fly us to the beach where we would begin our trip. When the weather ceiling lifted briefly, we ferried by floatplane in two trips to carry all the gear and passengers. There, on a beach beside Lake Grosvenor, we set up our tents that evening and assembled our folding aluminum and rubber canoes. Six people—five clients, plus our guide Allen—three canoes. After we tied off the canoes and ate dinner—away from our sleeping area—we locked our food and toiletries in stout, bear-resistant barrels and attached our three-wire battery-operated electric fence to aluminum poles, wrapping it in a tight-perimeter around our tents. Bears out. Humans in. We had come to see the world-famous Katmai brown bears, not get trampled by them in our sleep.

Our tents were pitched so close to each other the tent stakes touched. Instead of feeling cramped and claustrophobic, I felt like a child sleeping in her parents' bed while the wind raged outside. Safe, for now, with Allen, our strong, capable guide, teacher of survival skills in both the Arctic and Antarctic; with Betty, an Alaskan who had begun a new life after kidney and pancreas transplants; and with Carol and Gerry, who regularly escaped the comfort of their lives in New York City to plunge into the Alaskan wilderness. Tough, adventurous people, all.

The next morning after breaking camp, loading, and lashing everything down in the canoes, we pushed off. With frantic paddling we managed to dash across a choppy channel and reach a sheltered cove on the opposite shore. Too windy to continue, we made camp.

The following day, after paddling no more than two miles, we were forced off the lake again by fierce winds. The third day was much the same—loading gear, cinching it down, venturing out onto the lake, taking cover from the wind in the next cove. In three days on the water there were no other people on the lake besides a lone motorized boat that passed us yesterday. We covered three, maybe four miles at most through this land of jumbled granite, glacial moraine, and spongy moss. A tumultuous place. We had not even reached what was supposed to be our first camp.

Beneath the rich loam under our tents and feet lay volcanic ash, perhaps from Novarupta or any of the other major and minor explosions blasted from the Aleutian Range of volcanoes over the past 10,000 years. The Alutiiq people had traveled seasonally through this country for centuries, establishing temporary camps and, later, villages, harvesting the same rich resources as the bears—salmon, caribou, berries. With the 1912 explosion creating Novarupta, ash and pumice choked the lakes, killed the fish, and covered the land, forcing the people to abandon their homes and camps.

On the fourth day we woke to fog and tranquil waters. This was our chance. Allen hurried us through a breakfast of cereal, dried fruit, and coffee. We broke camp, loaded gear, tied it down, tightened our life jackets, and shoved off. Maybe we could make up time, reach what should have been our first camp, make Brooks Camp after all and see the bears.

We kept our heavily loaded canoes parallel to shore. Jim's strokes were precise, and even mine sliced the water expertly, exactly the way Allen showed me. Yes, this was the way I hoped it would be, skimming across smooth water, just like on our honeymoon.

After two hours of steady paddling, we docked on shore for a quick lunch as the fog began to evaporate, revealing the sharp gray spires of mountains on the opposite shore. We carried on. Jim and I took turns with Gerry and Betty's canoe in second position, while Allen and Carol remained in the lead. Periodically our three canoes drew close enough together to chat with our companions, then drifted away as Jim snapped pictures of the other canoes mirrored in the flat water. Paddle. Picture. Paddle. Picture. I became accustomed to this rhythm.

As our band of paddlers pressed close to the face of a shoreline cliff, three peregrine falcons shrieked, dove, and swooped at us (thankfully not as aggressively as the goshawk in Homer) until they were satisfied we were moving on. A pair of tundra swans passed above us, honking, quickly followed by a flock of six loons, voices not their usual forlorn cries, but sharp, more urgent calls as if signaling to each other to hurry up. Jim paused to unhook his camera from the metal strut, then captured another shot of the two canoes ahead of us.

A sudden blast of wind roiled the blue-gray surface of the lake. Waves immediately slammed against the gunwales, splashing over the side of the canoe. It was the assurance of Jim's composure that kept me from utter panic, even as the wind gathered force and blew us away from shore.

The canoe rocked in a sickening sideways motion. From his steering position in the stern, Jim attempted a pivot so the bow would head into the waves. But the wind threw us broadside. He shouted what I had trusted him never to shout—never imagined he would shout.

"I can't control it."

We were in trouble. My mind spun back to the Talachulitna River and my dive overboard. What was different about this crisis was the wind blowing us farther and farther from shore while the waves were mounting in size, as if we had taken this canoe out into the ocean. I wanted the same kind of calm, quick thinking in the face of calamity Jim had displayed on the Tal, but now our canoe swayed side-to-side, taking on water, threatening to flip. My paddling, made furious by his panic, turned us broadside to the waves.

"Stop! He shouted. "You're making it worse! I can't turn it around!"

As the wind shoved us further from shore, I took a sweep stroke, trying to help him wrest the boat from the force of the wind.

"Don't!" he screamed.

I pictured Jim's patched-up shoulder ripping apart, pins and screws prying loose from his frantic efforts to save us. And he wanted me to do nothing?

I glanced at our companions—Allen shouting orders to Carol as he expertly angled their canoe out of the wind's grip and pointed it toward shore; Gerry and Betty struggling to pivot their squat, bulky craft out of the brunt of the wind, shifting direction slightly, then pulling feverishly toward safety.

We were out there alone, a very long swim from shore, two bumbling, middle-aged canoers tossed by turbulent waters.

They died doing what they loved.

Bullshit.

Damn canoes, damn adventure, damn Jim for getting me into this. He managed a slight shift in the trajectory of the canoe. I paddled desperately, pulling back, lifting out, pulling back, repeating stroke after stroke, summoning all the energy my body had, heart beating so loudly I could hear it pounding in my ears. Deep exhales, sharp inhales, adrenaline pushing me to my limits. I couldn't keep it up much longer.

Finally—I had no idea how—the wind was at our backs and we were pointed toward safety. Rocks appeared in the clear shallow water. Sticks floating on top. Tiny fish. As we rammed into shore, I threw a trembling leg over the gunwale and nearly fell over as my boot hit the soft sand in the shallows. Staggering, I grabbed the bow and dragged it out of the water.

"Christ!" is all Jim said when he crawled out of the boat.

As he rubbed his shoulder I wanted to hug him, pledge my undying love, swear I would never make another water journey. Instead, he started unfastening straps, so I joined him in unloading gear.

We saved ourselves. Clumsy and unprepared, we survived.

On our fifth day the skies were clear, but the wind still ripped across the lake. Another shift in direction and acceleration of intensity. Waves pounded even our protected little bay.

We waited out the wind. Again.

"Give me rain, fog, and calm," said Allen as he gazed out on the swells rolling into shore.

We were still several miles from what was supposed to have been our first camp. If only we were expert canoers, if only we were younger and stronger, if only we were skilled enough to beat this wind. But in the interests of eluding death and celebrating a few more years together, I'd settle for this less-than-perfect camp and the comfort of land beneath my feet.

Sunlight filtered through the thick grass under the stunted birch and alders behind our camp. With no sign of the winds abating, I was eager to get moving on this bright autumn day. Jim said he wanted to fish, but I knew what he really wanted was to be left alone to wander the lakeshore, taking close-up pictures of leaves in water and lichen on rock, slabs of fungus on a tree, things I would pass by. I had learned in my years of traveling with Jim that he was happier when he could steal some time to himself, and I was happier with other people nearby in case he wandered off.

So we split up. Allen, Gerry, Carol, and I decided to climb. Betty would read in camp, and Jim would ramble wherever his eyes took him. I followed long-legged Allen. Behind me, Carol, barely one hundred pounds with short legs and a twisted spine, then Gerry, her stout husband, a full twelve inches taller than her. Allen walked slowly, planting his feet, making a path through brush reaching my knees but occasionally touching my chest. Bear trails were the only passages through the brush. Follow one and it disappeared or dead-ended in a tumble of wind-blown limbs. Beneath the thick mat of grass and fireweed lay hidden holes and hummocks. It was like walking on Arctic tundra except with tall vegetation hiding the uneven terrain. Frequently I looked behind me to see only the crown of Carol's red hat poking above the brush.

Allen changed course, beginning a long zigzag up the slope. At last we paused to rest on a flat, gray rock stenciled with green and white lichen. Out of the brush, the full force of the wind blasted us. From here we could trace our journey so far. The point where the bush plane dropped us off and we assembled our canoes. The small beach where we took refuge on our first day of paddling. The path of our pitifully scant progress. Tall grass hid the view of our camp below. We devoured a few granola bars, gulped some water and continued on.

Dipping down into a swale hidden from our view at camp, we made the final press to the crest of the ridge. At the top we planted our feet and leaned into the wind, quickly pulling hats, gloves, and windbreakers out of our packs. Below, we caught our first full view of the terrain. On one side of the ridge wind raked across the vast surface of Grosvenor Lake, creating swells and whitecaps. On the other, Naknek Lake, with its Bay of Islands, was a deep, churning blue. Far in the distance, the Savonoski River glinted with silvery braids. Beyond the roiling ponds and tiny lakes lay a chain of snow-capped mountains.

The reality of our task ahead sunk in—too much distance, not enough time. We would never make it to Brooks Camp. We would never see the bears the way we planned. Cold and disappointed, we turned back to camp, saying nothing but "Hey bear!" to announce our presence as we descended the ridge.

Back at camp Jim and I shared pictures—my crude shots taken from the top of the ridge, made blurry by the force of the wind and my inability to see without my glasses; his carefully composed images of a bright orange mushroom, a white feather lighting on a twig, green algae on water. I explained in detail the reasons why we would never have time to reach our destination. Jim seemed not to care.

The next day we woke to wind and fresh snow on the peaks across the lake, a surprise but not unusual in early fall. A layer of ice topped our water bucket. I couldn't get warm last night, despite sleeping in coat, hat, fleece pants, and wool socks.

Allen handed me a cup and I poured hot, dark coffee from the big blue metal pot. "We're stuck, right?" I asked. He nodded.

"We're not going to take the chance," he replied. He's had one traumatic canoe trip, he told me, and he wasn't about to lead us on another one.

I didn't ask for details because I didn't want to know. Jim and I had both noted the quiet sadness in Allen. No mystery as to its source—in the midst of his stories of climbing mountains and polar bear encounters in the Arctic, he had revealed that this summer—just weeks ago—he had lost two good friends in a small plane crash. Maybe this trip was a distraction for him. Maybe it was a reminder of the thin thread by which we all stay alive.

We six started as strangers, but we had been together long enough to have measured each other's mettle under stress. Though Carol and Gerry seemed at first like privileged East Coast urbanites, I learned to respect their wilderness experience in Alaska and other remote locations around the globe. And choppy waters were insignificant compared to what Betty had been through waiting for and finally receiving a new organ.

This journey's gift to us now was time—no pressure, no need to muster courage or spectacular physical prowess. I sat in the sun, read, wrote in my journal, made crude sketches of the craggy ridges and the deep green valley across the lake. Streams flowed down several flanks. What was up there? If we could hike the slopes, would we reach an alpine lake?

I ventured to the beach, where I joined Jim in wandering, weaving new memories into those we had brought from our pasts even before our lives intertwined. For me, this meant traveling with my family, my sister and me in the back of our old station wagon, our destination a beach like the one we walked now (except we could reach it by road). When we arrived at whatever spot my dad thought would have the best fishing, we'd unload, set up camp, build a fire. Then, as I sat on a log or rock, I'd pinch myself to make sure I wasn't dreaming, because being outside, in the woods, away from town was so thrilling I could barely believe my good luck. I have never quite lost that feeling. Maybe that was what attracted me to Jim.

We stole a kiss and embraced behind granite boulders. Middle school love. A pause in the ordinary, far away from the familiar. In this moment all of our choices felt right.

After consulting with Gerry, Carol, and Betty, we convinced Allen to call his boss by satellite phone and request the flight service pick us up here and fly us to Brooks Camp. We still had a chance to see the bears. We would gladly pay extra. Allen called the owner of the company, then the bush pilot who dropped us off days ago. Yes, he could pick us up. If the wind died down.

Early the next morning we were still in our tents sleeping when Betty called out to us.

"Get up, everyone. Allen says we're moving."

Our destination: a deeper, less rocky cove where the pilot could land his floatplane safely without worrying about the pontoons hitting any rocks or trees beneath the water.

I popped my head out of the sleeping bag and nudged Jim. A faint light filtered through the tent window. A strange silence. No wind. When we crawled out of the tent, the unruffled surface of the lake reflected a brilliant orange glow rising between a notch in the mountains in front of us. But we had no time to savor the view. We had to make our move during this window of good, windless weather. While Allen fixed coffee and oatmeal, we broke down our tents, stuffed gear into waterproof bags, and began loading the canoes. We would have to paddle back the way we came to reach a deeper bay, and a safer landing for the plane. It would take two trips by plane for all of us and our gear. With trembling hands and quaky stomach, I helped Jim lift the heavy bear-proof barrels into the bottom of the canoe, then packed the rest of the gear around them. All I could think of was wind—how it could sneak up, vicious and relentless, blowing us out to the middle of the lake, never letting us go. Beside me, Jim scurried around the canoe, rearranging bags, tightening straps, lashing the load securely. If he was worried, he kept it hidden.

No more time for my obsessing. We grabbed the sides of the canoe and launched it into the tranquil water. With Allen and Betty in the lead, Jim and I paddled flawlessly along a shoreline of bright red and yellow fall foliage, retracing the route bringing us here. Had we missed the colors in our panic to reach a safe harbor, or had autumn progressed so quickly while we waited out the wind?

Without the wind we became a floating team, relishing the beauty around us, strong, competent, confident. In a little over an hour we reached the cove we had passed three days earlier. Deeper, wider, less chance of crashing against submerged rocks than last night's camp spot, it was a good place to land a floatplane and taxi out again.

Privacy, at last. Ironically, it was in the midst of the bustling village of Brooks Camp where we had a chance to be alone. Our group had scattered to the far ends of the campground. Jim and I pitched our tent in an extravagant amount of space, and no one paid attention to us. Still, even with the space, after seven days without any other people and the quiet of nature, the activity was overwhelming. We were surrounded by a clatter of different languages, people hurrying to catch buses, cooking in the kitchen shelters, storing their gear in designated sheds, a continual procession of tourists dressed in the finest European outdoor gear money could buy, as well as Alaskans in muddy, well-worn rain gear, scuffed up hiking shoes, and faded backpacks. Brooks Camp is an international destination. It contains a campground surrounded by a stout electrified fence, a lodge with basic services, a visitor center, a floatplane dock, a bus for trips along the short road leading to the Land of Ten Thousand Smokes, the sparse volcanic landscape created by the 1912 eruption. The year of our trip some 11,000 people visited the camp alone, with around 26,000 total to Katmai National Park. Now, at Labor Day, we were between late runs of salmon and the end of season.

In that small, always-bustling community, Jim and I were free to gossip about our fellow travelers and snip at each other. I was too slow fastening the tent hooks to the poles; he was impatient staking out the rain fly. I had lost his headlamp; he had left it in his sleeping bag. It was as if we had been on our guard those past seven days and were at last free to be ourselves. Yet no one would know if we snuggled up in our tent, made love, took a nap.

Our group met at the campground gate to hike the trail to Brooks Falls—there was safety in numbers since bears had the right-of-way everywhere. We reached the lower viewing platform, called the Riffles, where sow grizzlies often fish with their young cubs, avoiding the large males at the falls. No bears were fishing there. We continued along the raised walkway to the two-tiered platform overlooking the falls, the lower deck at eye-level to the river and the upper with a longer view of the falls. Only two other visitors were on the upper deck when we arrived—a man with a long, heavy-looking camera lens and a woman with binoculars. Our group spread out along the railing. The falls were empty. A few more people arrived. No one spoke out loud but there were whispers, murmurs, muffled coughs, and quiet shuffles, an atmosphere of reverence like church or the hush of an audience right before a symphony begins. All of us waited excitedly for the bears—all except Jim. He found plenty to photograph as the mergansers performed in the shallows along the shore. Diving ducks, they raced through the water, herding fish, snatching them, then darting off to swallow them before other ducks had a chance to steal their dinners.

A dark shape moved from below the deck. Whispered *oohs*. Clicks of cameras and cell phones, the lengthening of tripods. A large male grizzly sauntered through the water, then snagged a bright red spawning salmon from the shallows, ripped it apart, and devoured it. Glancing over his shoulder, he edged downstream.

Another bear appeared in the tall grass across the river. As he lumbered toward the water, the enormity of his body came into full view. A sumo wrestler of a bear, his belly sagged to mere inches above the ground. Jim mobilized, taking pictures from every angle as the bear peered over the falls, then eased his body into the cascades. Like a fat man in a Jacuzzi, he let the water beat up against his belly, occasionally grabbing a salmon and taking a bite out of it, then letting it drop. He was king of the falls. As he luxuriated, so did we, rewarded for our long storm-tossed journey. We dallied until twilight faded, then hiked back to camp.

It was time to leave. We had stacked our gear on the beach where the floatplane would land. Naturally, I couldn't find Jim. I backtracked to the lodge, to the platform at the river, to the floating bridge, to the campground, to the gift shop, to the trail along the beach. After thirty years I had nearly learned to give up worrying, but there was nothing I could do to make him tell me where he was going or when he would be back. Here, at least, I was surrounded by people coming and going from the floatplane dock. I sat with the rest of our group, scanning the beach for Grandma Bear. This was her beat. Park rangers said she had been claiming this section of real estate for the past twenty-five years. It was not the best fishing spot, but it was steady, away from the big males, and there was plenty of soft sand for napping. As a grandmother, I understood her desire to steer clear of the jockeying for supremacy at the big fishing hole, and the relief of not having to worry about child bearing or child tending any longer. I too would like to nap here on the beach in the warm autumn sun, but I know better than to risk dozing in the path of a cranky bear. And there was that nagging worry—what's become of Jim?

From behind us, he emerged from the alders, alongside the trail leading to the campground.

Me: "Where were you?"

Him: "I saw the coolest thing."

He offered his bright red camera to me, scrolling through the pictures to share what he found. He was that schoolboy back in the swamp.

He plucked a pumice stone from the beach, remnant of the pyroclastic explosion once choking this entire lake, and tossed it in the water. Together, we watched as it floated away.

"Let's come back again," he said. "There's a lot we haven't seen."

To this, I had no response. He was right. In my mind, I was already planning our return. Next time, we'd fly—skip the water, spend more time with the bears. It's the smart way to go, easier by far than tangling with wind and waves.

Skip the water? Who was I kidding?

Chapter Twenty-One

White marble crosses and Stars of David fanned out across the precisely groomed lawn. White on green. No families gathered at the headstones. No messy floral bouquets to disturb the order and symmetry.

As we stepped off the bus, a weight settled on my shoulders. Dread, melancholy—I'm not sure which. I hated cemeteries, especially military ones. Young people honored in death, yet so easily sacrificed in life. A few days before this on our Best of Europe tour, we had made a pilgrimage to Dachau, the first Nazi concentration camp. The day before, a local guide had led us on a walking tour of Munich, tracing Hitler's rise to power, paralleling those events with some of the current politics in our own country—the rise of white supremacy, police brutality, the lure of authoritarianism. I'd had enough of fascism, war, and death.

The stop at the Florence American Cemetery and Memorial was not on our scheduled itinerary.

This extravagant journey had been my idea, a gathering of three generations to celebrate our daughter and son-in-law's twentieth wedding anniversary, our grandson Cason's eighteenth birthday, granddaughter Carly's sixteenth, and my seventieth. I hoped a glimpse of the wider world would be my legacy to them. I thought if I could just hold my family close one more time—what? They would remember me? Thank me? I wasn't sure.

Eric Erickson, the developmental psychologist, believed the task of the last phase of life is to reconcile integrity with despair. If we look back on our lives and feel a sense of accomplishment then we will feel complete, that our life had value. If we look back and feel guilty because we don't believe we have met our goals, then we will feel hopeless. The ultimate aim of this phase is *wisdom*. I felt neither wise nor hopeless, nor ready to declare this the final phase of my life.

We started the tour in Paris—twenty-eight of us, our family of six, twenty other tourists, plus our Dutch guide and driver—traveling by bus for fourteen days through France, Switzerland, Germany, and Italy, ending up in Rome.

Perhaps our young Dutch guide thought a stop at the Florence American Cemetery during the Italian phase of our tour would be a fitting example of both the worst and best of the continent. Maybe as Americans we would appreciate the generosity of the Italian government in donating this land to the United States for a cemetery. A way to honor the lives of the American soldiers who died to liberate their country from the Nazis during World War II. I would rather have carried on to Rome.

We stood on the concrete steps beneath a wall filled with plaques. The cemetery docent pointed to a statue on a pylon high above us, a woman grasping olive branches, poised as if flying. "The Spirit of Peace," he said.

In the distance, a smaller sculpture rose, an American soldier standing guard over the graves. Peace and war, at opposite ends of the manicured field. In between, some 4,400 fallen fighters who gave their lives to halt the spread of fascism.

Here was one of those places, the guide explained—the last great push to roust the German army from Italy. On the ground and in the air the Allies joined forces to squeeze the Axis troops farther and farther north, a crucial step toward breaching their heavily fortified defenses along the Apennines Mountains. Those American soldiers who fell here were mostly the air crews—pilots, bombers, gunners. The guide paused to catch his breath.

A fragment of memory shook loose in my brain—from a long-lost photo album, a black and white picture of my dad. Young and thin with thick black hair, he stood in front of the plane in which he was a gunner, flying missions over France and Italy. Not long before he died, he took Mom to see the cities he had visited, the places he helped liberate—Paris, Rome, and Florence. Here, I realized. He fought here. In these skies. Over this land.

The docent gestured to a massive stone panel directly behind us, engraved with hundreds of names. The missing—never found, never returned—some 1,400 of them. My mind strayed to exploding planes, their occupants spilling from the sky with the aircraft, traces of matter becoming rain, wind, soil, wildflowers, trees, and the river below.

Dad's plane was shot down. I didn't know where. Was it the plane in the picture I remember or another? Did it crash, or did they land safely in a damaged plane? Were the details too painful for him to talk about, or was I too self-absorbed to care? He was no longer around to fill in the gaps in my hazy memory.

He could easily have been in one of these graves, or his name carved in stone, one of those missing in action. But he survived, returned home, married my mother, brought up three daughters who raised four children of their own.

My chin quivered. Tears spilled down my cheeks. As the rest of the group walked quietly among the graves, I hung back, ashamed of my tears, ashamed of not recognizing this place. Ashamed that until now, I had not thought of my father once during this trip. He died thirty-one years ago. This was the first time I had shed tears for him.

Buried memories flooded back: the two of us setting up a tent in the backyard so my friends and I could camp outside, the tenderness with which he cared for my mom when she was bedridden. Tears now coursed down my neck as I recognized how arrogant I was, forgetting those gentle moments in favor of living a life different from his—more intellectual, worldly, exciting than the one I believed he had lived. I was uninterested in the lessons my father wanted to convey and in the few stories he was willing to tell. I wanted to make my own way. He had dropped out of high school; I was determined to attend college. He worked with his hands; I wanted nothing to do with his kind of work. My young adult world of college, anti-war protests, and the sexual revolution was as alien to him as the music and culture of my grandkids are to me. We argued through those years: me full of myself, discovering new geographic and intellectual landscapes, so much more sophisticated than that of my family; him wanting me to understand what he had fought for, the price of my comfortable life. I didn't know what else he really wanted from me, but I was certain I'd fallen short of what he thought I should become.

I had no way of knowing how battle had changed him. He was an anxious man, an alcoholic, a man often not at peace. I didn't know how much of his addiction stemmed from growing up in a family of ten kids with not enough food to eat, or how much came from what he went through in the war. But I knew every time our family traveled by air, my father transformed into an angry, agitated man I didn't recognize, screaming at airline staff when schedules went awry, tossing luggage, swearing at my mother. As a child I found his behavior at those times both frightening and confusing. Had he been thinking of the missions he flew in the war? I doubt he would have made the connection between his war trauma and this outsized response to a situation in which he had no control. The Vietnam War raged throughout my high school and college years. Men returned from battle broken physically and mentally. It has taken decades to develop effective ways of treating those scars. Men of Dad's generation did not have access to that kind of care.

Dad enlisted in the Army Air Corps at seventeen, a year younger than my grandson Cason today, a boy who did not even shave at that age. Dad's parents gave their grudging permission, he had said. He had earlier dropped out of high school to help support the family. His absence, and that of his older brother, also fighting, must have caused considerable hardship, especially since their father worked away from home for months at a time, moving from one job to another.

While I was growing up, Dad would grow depressed at Christmas. He hated Christmas music. It reminded him of the war, how they played old songs and carols in the barracks, making him desperately homesick. I discounted his memories, angry he drank so much more during the holidays.

Once I found a stash of letters Dad had sent to my mom while he was away at war, written on tiny bits of wispy paper, sections of sentences blacked out by censors. The care and longing of two young people in love embarrassed me. I put the letters away and never looked at them again. If we as children allowed ourselves to see how vulnerable, how human our parents are, how could we ever break away? I saw the same in my grandchildren. During his early teens, Cason challenged, goaded, pushed until his father blew up and yelled. Carly screaming, crying, blaming her mother for whatever went wrong in her life. This was the hard work of leaving the nest. If we are lucky, we all still love each other.

I glanced back at the rows of white on green, thinking of the seventeen-year-old boy whose life had been changed forever by what happened here, his youth given over to the arrogance of war so I could live safe and free. He must have been hurt I did not appreciate how he managed to survive, how he managed to keep going.

I rejoined my family, none of whom knew their history was bound to this ground. My father died long before my grandchildren were born.

"You never knew your great-grandfather," I said. "He fought here."

I told them what I knew, what I wished I knew. My story. Our story.

Chapter Twenty-Two

Kim saved up all her cash for this trip-of-a-lifetime to the Arctic. Ever since we touched down in our fat-tired bush plane two days ago, she has been like a teenager in love. She couldn't sleep, eat, or settle down. She acted like she was the first person to be left breathless by the brief gold and scarlet splash of fall in the Arctic.

We old-timers allowed her this love-at-first-sight romance with the land because she reminded us of why we live in Alaska— and why we had chosen to head north in this fickle season, when the waning days of summer could be obliterated at any moment by a deep freeze or snowstorm.

She stepped upslope and snapped a picture.

"Women picking berries," Kim captioned us.

High above our camp on the Canning River, we were harvesting a patch of late-blooming blueberries overlooked by hungry bears, squirrels, and voles. Plump, tiny berries, as purple as dusty plums, clustered beneath crimson leaves no bigger than my pinkie's fingernail, growing just inches from the spongy ground. Eagerly, we popped them into our mouths. Aged by the summer's constant light and now the first frost, these berries were sweeter than any fat, uniform, store-bought berries in their plastic cages. We four women savored this unexpected gift, an excuse to pause in our laboring up the mountain.

Nancy, one of our two guides on this eight-day trip, gently pulled the berries from their fragile stems. She squatted, knees together, feet splayed apart in a pretzel pose my rusty joints no longer achieved. Her cracked, dirt-lined hands were topographic maps of past wanderings, from the Arctic to Antarctica and points between.

When we had wrested all the ripe berries from their stubby bushes, Nancy rose and hoisted her duct-tape-patched rain pants up over her scrawny hips and headed up the mountain with Kim. They were mountain women. Kim lived in a cabin high in the Rockies and Nancy, only days before joining the trip as our guide, had completed a solo trek across Iceland. Deb, though, had no need to push farther. She hunkered into a shallow depression in the damp tundra.

"I'm going to write in my journal," she said. "Or maybe take a nap."

I was curious to find out what was on the other side of this mountain, so I followed Kim and Nancy. Like a little sister, I tried to keep up. I was at least ten years older than each of them, though, and after a few minutes I tucked into a swale to catch my breath. By the time I started moving again, Kim and Nancy were out of sight, their voices faint burbles drifting back on the wind. The higher I trudged, the worse I knew my knees would feel on the trip down. I stopped briefly to catch a picture of our tents below—multi-colored eggs nesting in the ruddy tundra—then I backtracked to Deb.

Deb and I met in a nature-writing course several years earlier. We shared a sisterhood of bad knees, alcoholic fathers, quirky mothers, and an obsession with the written word. Deb's motto was "no stinking trees" and this was her kind of place. Raised in Colorado, stationed with the National Park Service at outposts as disparate as Florida's Dry Tortugas and International Falls, Minnesota, Deb was happiest at latitudes with clear views of the horizon. We had traveled as far as the deserts of Namibia together. There were no more seasoned or unflappable travel companions than Deb and her husband Jay, who was fishing somewhere below us on the river right now.

There were also no prissy women on this trip, not like the crew from back East on another Arctic trip a few years ago along the Kongakut River. Those three women emerged from their tents each morning fully made-up and perfectly coiffed, looking like models for a trendy outdoor clothing catalog. I was elated to now be in the company of women not afraid of dirty hair, stinky clothes, wet feet, and squatting in the willows. Of my sisters, daughter, grandchildren, cousins, aunts, and uncles, I was the only one crazy enough to enjoy such a trip. In a strange sort of way, I had my mother to thank for this. The berry-picking accident when we were new to Alaska, her mysterious illness not long after, her subsequent failed pregnancies, the chaos engulfing our family when my grandparents died. Not knowing if I could depend on her freed me to discover my own path.

Deb and I scrunched down into the soft tundra, plundering our bags of trail mix and jotting notes in our respective journals until clouds shrouded the sun, our backsides grew numb, and our leg muscles seized up. Before we left on this trip, Deb and I each had our knees shot up with some magical lubricant that temporarily delayed a major overhaul. It allowed us to climb this mountain, crouch, and hoist our butts in and out of our tents, but it offered no elixir of youth on a long downhill run.

As mist drifted in from the Arctic Ocean, we reached into our packs for raincoats. We shivered, shook out stiff legs, and began the long descent, leaving Nancy and Kim to discover what lay beyond the peak above us. We hurried as much as possible over spiky-headed tundra tussocks, trying to coax warmth back into cold feet and hands, headed for camp and something hot to drink, our hard-earned berries safe in our bellies.

Chapter Twenty-Three

We had made up our minds, Jim and I. We would not succumb to stagnation. We would not be content gazing wistfully at objects collected over our lifetimes. We would not be artifacts of our past, nor leave our heirs a crumbling cabin or a houseful of objects they would just throw away.

During the COVID-19 pandemic we were forced to take a good look at our surroundings and our mortality. We decided to make the house where we had lived for thirty-odd years shiny and new, pretending we had unlimited years ahead of us. We would finally renovate the first floor of our house, the only portion never benefiting from the major remodeling the rest of the structure had received over the years. It would mean removing everything from all the first-story rooms, tearing down a wall and building a new one, covering the old 1970's "popcorn" type ceiling with new drywall, and applying fresh paint to all the rooms.

But first, we had to excavate.

We started with the Franklin wood stove. No fires had burned in its belly for more than a decade, so digging it out of the niche in our family room where it had lived since the house was built forty years ago should have been easy. Placed on a tile platform, the massive chunk of cast iron took up one whole wall, making the room appear to be one long hallway. The Franklin was a workhorse, though, heating our two-story house enough to keep the pipes from freezing and bursting, and providing a hot surface for cooking in case of natural disasters and power outages. But it was greedy, burning too hot and too fast, gobbling up wood, dumping its heat extravagantly into the family room, robbing the rest of the house of warmth.

In the early years of the house and our family we didn't mind giving the stove what it demanded—lots of wood, careful calibration of its damper, old rugs to cover the spots where embers leaped out while reloading, and frequent sweeping to discard its ample accumulations of ash. With plenty of embers and constant tending, it could simmer a big pot of soup all day and yield a week of meals. We were hardy Alaskans then, foraging for wood, chopping down our own Christmas trees, making granola, camping, skiing to backcountry cabins, careening down sledding hills on giant inner tubes. In our family room, all furnishings, art, entertainment, and human activity revolved around the cast iron behemoth. Its double doors, each with an embossed pine tree, opened wide to accommodate large logs, preferably slow-burning birch, though other woods would do. But then our daughter grew up and left, and so did our grandchildren. Age and injuries took their toll, and we weren't so hardy anymore. Besides, home generators were on sale at Costco.

The removal of this artifact required two strong men who arrived one afternoon to wrest the Franklin from its base, lift it onto a four-wheeled cart, guide it gingerly through the narrow gap between the wall and washer in our laundry room, and then through the garage and onto the driveway. There, they wrapped a towing strap around its middle, lowered the arm of a crane, and hoisted the monster into the bed of their truck. Cash was exchanged, hands were shaken, and the Franklin rode out into the cold. Goodbye smoke, ash, singed mittens, and burnt fingers.

As we counted our cash and good fortune, we looked at what remained: a dangling chimney pipe, scattered bits of concrete, a square of naked plywood where the stove had been anchored to its tile floor. We asked ourselves what we had done.

With Jim briefly out of town, I donned a pair of paint-spattered jeans and a frayed sweatshirt. Better to start the next job by myself. All of the artwork on the walls of the first floor had to be removed and stored somewhere upstairs in preparation for the construction. If we tackled this together, we would surely argue over each piece of art—what to keep, what to toss away.

Clouds of dust escaped from shelves and picture frames as I removed each article from its long-time home. Bright squares left on dingy walls, dark circles on tabletops otherwise faded by the sun. As I handled each object, I wondered how long it had been since I had really looked at it. Despite my best intentions, each work of art triggered a memory and a reckoning. *Where did it come from? Why do we keep it?* The fierce black goshawk with scarlet background, a trade with an artist friend for one of Jim's photos. The pen-and-ink lynx with driftwood frame, origin unknown. The Inupiat drum with painted wood frog, a gift from Jim's friends for his fiftieth birthday. A small square of green and purple wool hanging by a twig, our granddaughter's first attempt at knitting. A woman's torso carved by a long-lost friend. Faded prayer flags from Bhutan. More and more and more.

I carried these items upstairs and stacked them according to my arbitrary sorting system: those I loved, those I hated and would be happy to get rid of, and those I knew my husband would never let go. After several hours I had become a curator in an art museum, tediously examining each work of art, taking too much time, revisiting old travels and people long gone. Finally, I had removed all adornments from two rooms downstairs and stacked them upstairs.

Now that I had started, I was overwhelmed by the enormity of this task, the volume of stuff we had collected, the need to do something with it while we remade the first floor of the house.

Maybe this was all a mistake. Instead of renovating we should have been downsizing, selling the house, moving into a condo, settling into our rocking chairs. But that would mean leaving the neighborhood we loved, the trails, the house almost perfect. We had to push through this phase; I was sure it would get easier.

No children slept in the downstairs bedroom any longer. A bed, rocking chair, table, a few odds and ends. We would make quick work of it. Keep the rocking chair, get rid of the table, sort the objects lining the ledge running around the entire room.

A once-white stuffed dog with a bandaged leg sat on the ledge where it was abandoned a decade ago. I lifted the animal from its home and vacuumed the spiderwebs from behind it. Whose dog was it? Granddaughter or grandson? Or did it belong to their mother? I remembered a scraped knee—a fall off a bike or a tumble while leaping to catch a ball—one Band-Aid for the crying child and one for the toy dog. I held the animal to my nose, and instead of the sweet childhood scent I remember, I smelled dust and mildew. The child who once grasped this toy would now have to find grownup sources of comfort. Maybe it was Carly who had stuck the Band-Aid on the dog so securely. At an early age she was fascinated with the body, wanting to become a healer. Now she was away at college, well on her way to that goal. A moment's thought: *Should I wash the dog and pass it forward to another generation?* No, it would likely fall apart and was probably full of toxic substances. I hesitated, then tossed it into the black trash bag.

The trundle bed, which could convert from a single to twins to a king, no longer served a purpose. The kids who needed separate beds when they spent the night, who fought each time about who got which bed, now had to deal with college roommate conflicts. I wondered who would help Cason through his search for whatever Neptune he needed to find now.

The levers of the old bed, always cranky, now barely budged. Its clunky wrought-iron headboard, extending around two sides of the bed to keep children from rolling out, made changing sheets an acrobatic activity.

Jim had placed an ad for the bed on Craigslist, and the

next day a middle-aged couple, desperate for a bed that could fit in a tiny spot, drove forty miles to take it off our hands. Four of us struggled, using tools and muscle power, to disassemble the metal frame. With the pieces loaded into the truck and tied with straps and bungee cords, we waved goodbye. Only then did it sink in that the child-tending phase of our lives had officially ended.

In the blank space once occupied by the bed we found grooves, divots, and rust spots on the carpet, scuffs on the wall, an Uno card, and golf-ball-sized clumps of dust. We could now turn to the mess jammed inside the room's closet. Sleeping bags, wetsuits, summer clothes, blankets, sheets, suits no longer fitting, and dresses long out of style. More sorting: send to Goodwill, move upstairs to store, throw away.

With the contents of the closet removed, we tore out the old shelves, never quite wide enough, and clothing rods, never quite high enough. Beneath them we found traces of paint from previous epochs. Lime, the color of the bedroom when we moved in during Elisha's elementary school years. Pale pink, from her girly adolescent phase. Neutral beige from the on-again, off-again living-at-home college years. Finally, dusky white for our grandchildren's sleepover years. Memories spilled out with the flying dust. Scents of perfume, hairspray, sweat, dog, and purloined pizza. And sounds: nightmare cries of *Mommy*! Slammed doors and angry words later regretted. The thrum and thud of heavy metal music. The tap, tapping of boys at the window, beckoning our daughter for a midnight escape. The soft sighs of grandchildren safe asleep in their mother's old bedroom.

***

Three, four-drawer metal file cabinets occupied one corner of Jim's office. Two of them contained hundreds of slide photos in plastic sleeves hanging from folders. Jim had never lost his photographic eye or his passion for taking pictures throughout all his career changes. Photo exhibits, magazine stories and covers, contests. Jim's high-quality art reached a broad audience. These originals were stored, along with the images of our lives together—travels, friends, family, celebrations, disasters—in the drawers of these four heavy steel cabinets. Hidden, safe, unorganized, and mostly forgotten. For years he had struggled with what to do with them. Spend time digitizing and categorizing, leave them all in their little sleeves seen by no one, or get rid of them? Slide projectors had gone the way of VHS tapes and print film. Elisha politely declined to accept the slides as her inheritance, saying, "I don't know what I would do with them."

Some slides had been made into prints and subsequently wound up in birthday or anniversary albums, and others from some of Jim's art exhibits and contests had been printed, mounted, and framed and were now stored upstairs, but we never got around to spending the time and money to turn the rest of them into accessible images. Neither one of us wanted to take time revisiting the past this way when the time ahead was limited.

Now, as we worked to dismantle Jim's desk and get ready to move the cabinets, he reached a decision point on his photos: move, digitize, or dump. While I tossed paper recycling into a bin, Jim stared at the cabinets. I was sure he remembered the weeks after his father died, digging through picture albums—loose snapshots and negatives of photos his father had taken, people and places we could not identify. In the end we discarded all but a handful, those containing people Jim and his brother Paul recognized and cared about.

After several moments sitting immobile in his chair, he stood up, opened a drawer, reached for a sleeve of slides, and tossed it.

Stop! I wanted to shout. *This was too final. Couldn't we save some of them?* He was throwing away not just representations of his unique view of the world, his art, but also the history of our lives together, the places we traveled, how we lived, what small space we occupied on this planet. Without the pictures, those windows to the past would be gone.

"Are you sure you want to do this?" I asked.

"I haven't looked in those drawers in years. No one will want this stuff when I'm gone," he said.

The photos were his art, his craft, and his records of our family history. This was his decision to make. Our lives were much more than pictures. When we were both gone, our daughter would have no need to cling to these artifacts. What she would remember of us would not lie in little squares of film.

He filled the trash bin, once, twice, again, and again.

At least we had no attachment to the functional beige and brown flecked carpet, a remnant of an event we'd rather not have lived.

One frigid February day, decades ago, while we were away on vacation, thieves entered our house, ransacked the place, threw an odd assortment of our possessions into my car, drove off with it, and left the garage door open. As if car theft and robbery weren't enough, the open door caused the pipes to freeze, then they burst and flooded the downstairs. A homecoming we will never forget.

The aftermath, in the dead cold of winter: sucking up the water with a commercial vacuum; ripping up the soggy carpet; drying all with giant fans; replacing pipes; patching the wall where the break occurred; quickly replacing the old carpet with a cheap, new, available replacement. Years later, the inexpensive fabric we had been walking on for all those years, with its stains, grime, and footpaths, was a painful reminder of that quick decision. We would replace it with durable, waterproof, laminate flooring. It's the new trend, Elisha said, easier to clean, better for resale. "I'm not worried about resale," said Jim. He planned to die here, I supposed, and leave the resale to me, or more likely, to her when we were both too feeble to manage the place.

I assumed the construction crew would handle the carpet demolition. Aside from generating more dust, its removal should have been painless. Tear it out, take it away. But when Jim asked our contractor what they would do with the used carpet, he said dump it in the landfill. There, it would poison the ground and never decay. I didn't want to think about that. Jim's idea was to rip it up ourselves and give it away. My environmental conscience said, *Don't pollute the landfill.* My back said, *No way am I yanking up that carpet.*

As it turned out, Jim had already placed a *Free Carpet* ad on Craigslist and received several calls. A potential taker was already on his way from Willow, about seventy-five miles north of Anchorage, to take a look at it. When the man arrived he said nothing as he walked through each room, dodging ladders, tools, disassembled window blinds, and other debris, examining the carpet. In less than five minutes, he looked up, nodded, and said, "I'll take it," promising to return in a few days with a friend who owned a truck. I worried the man was casing our home to rob later, though nothing he saw in his quick tour would give him reason to think we had anything of value.

Jim had faith the man was honest and would keep his word about returning, so he began slicing the carpet along the edges. Following behind reluctantly, I pulled the fabric away from the tacks and glue. It *was* back-breaking work, but I assumed we were just pulling the edges to make the man's work easier.

Not so. Jim kept going, surging ahead of me as usual, tugging the carpet away from the floor, inch by inch. I could have been stubborn and let him do it all himself, but I would have just felt guilty and worried about the toll on his back and shoulder. So I helped. Beneath the mottled green and yellow pad we found fine gray grit, dead bugs, and, finally, the concrete slab of our foundation, splotched with brown and red paint and speckles of white plaster, tracks of whomever built this house some forty years ago. We heard rumors the house was originally built by volunteers hoping to use the building as a church until they could raise enough money for a proper one. Did they place their hopes for salvation and a new community into the effort to erect this structure? Did we benefit from their benedictions? I only knew the house, the neighborhood, the trails, and the shelter it provided had blessed us for all these years, despite the house payments nearly breaking us in the beginning, back when Jim had started his business and I was unemployed. I thought of the years of comfort the house had given us, how we had moved in as a young family, raised a daughter, and then mentored and loved two grandchildren as they reached adulthood. Now we were elders in a neighborhood with a new generation of children. What will the next owners wonder about us, the crazy changes we had made, the yard sculptures Jim created with scrap metal and other cast-offs, the way we let the lawn grow feral?

Before I knew it, not only had we rolled up the carpet in each room, but Jim convinced me the bulky, awkward rolls were in the way of removing doors and making way for the carpenters.

"Let's move it all to the garage, so he can just pull up, load it, and take it away," Jim said.

With much yelling and swearing, we maneuvered the carpet rolls one by one onto a wheeled cart, squeezed them through the laundry room, and dumped them onto the garage floor.

The next day the man arrived as promised—with friend and truck—and loaded the rolls into the truck bed. The work seemed almost worthwhile now that it was done, and I was forced to admit to myself Jim had more persistence than I did.

Jim and I stood beside each other in the driveway as the two men got ready to drive off with their prize. The friend leaned his head out the window. "They really appreciate this," I heard him whisper to Jim, "They live in a shop with a concrete floor. This will make their lives so much better."

At last, the preparation work was complete and the construction crew could take over. One night, after they had gone home, I descended the stairs into the exposed cavity of our house. Beams, bones, and central nervous system—heat, water, electrical wires. Stripped of the personal, it could be anyone's house, small and unremarkable. A place where anyone could live, love, fight, raise children, and move on. I felt a moment of regret over what we had erased, our familiar surroundings, our past. And yet also joy. My shoes clicked across the bare concrete floor. I tapped a little dance, steps echoing back to me from the bare walls. Jim and I would begin again, just the two of us. What would we create in this old/new place? I didn't know how many more years we had, but we would surround ourselves with the colors, textures, and objects we valued, including a few cherished artifacts from our excavation. The black goshawk. The Inupiat drum. The poster from our river trip down the Grand Canyon. Our granddaughter's ragged attempt at knitting.

Epilogue

Every winter I lifted the skate skis from their rack in the garage, dusted them off, had a new base wax applied at the local sporting goods store. I had skate skied two or three times, never progressing beyond the beginner level. Then I reverted back to my old fishscale skis.

One day, while laboring up a parallel track with my clunky old fish scales, a man skate-skied up the hill past me. He was not a young kid. Back bent from age (and possibly arthritis), he looked eighty or more. Slowly, smoothly, he carved neat X's in the snow, no wasted motion, nothing holding him back.

What kept me from achieving this seemingly effortless synchrony? Fear.

Only one thing would work to overcome it. Practice.

A decade before, I was shopping at an after-Christmas sale and stopped at a rack of skate skis. Price reduced, and an even better bargain, the clerk said, if you bought the boots and poles with them. My gaze landed on a pair of candy-apple red boots that said *Racing* across the side. Who was I kidding?

"Thanks," I told him, "but I'm not ready."

I wandered into the women's clothing section and rummaged through the sweaters. I talked to myself: *You don't need another pair of skis. You're too old to learn another style of skiing. Forget it.*

Going to the coffee shop next door, I grabbed a beverage, then returned to the skis. There was no good reason to buy those skis except for the movie playing in my head, the one of me sashaying down the trail, floating on snow, legs and arms in perfect harmony.

I bought them: skinny skate skis, red boots.

Jim had no desire to learn a new skiing technique at this phase of his life, so I was on my own. I took a few lessons and discovered skate skiing was much harder than diagonal skiing. The skis were faster than my fishscales and the technique was more demanding, more pushing than shuffling, with none of the drag slowing down no-wax skis. More than that, I was afraid. At the top of a hill I froze, remembering the young woman I once was at the top of the downhill ski run. But I went down anyway. I fell often, landing with a hard thwack, and took a week or three to recover. Other times I achieved a small triumph, scaling a hill, then snowplowing down without falling. I clung to the fantasy that one day I would master the dance on skate skis other people seemed to achieve so easily.

Still, I never lost the fear.

In a winter during the pandemic years, snow fell repeatedly and the temperature held at freezing or below. Perfect conditions for skiing, but they might not last. Climate change now brought more frequent thaws. Good snow called with an urgency to use it while it lasted.

I loaded my skinny skis, boots, and poles in the back of my car and headed for the trail. After a string of overcast, never-quite-daylight days, and the social isolation of the pandemic, clear skies made the snow shine brighter and the frost-laden trees appear more luminous, as if I had put on a newer, sharper pair of glasses and saw a clearer version of the world. Even the air smelled purer.

At seventy-two, I warmed up like an old car in the cold, gears stiff and cranky. I practiced my technique on a trail where high school and college ski teams would not zoom past, irritated at this slow-moving object obstructing their path. Legs, hips, and arms complained with the first few slices of skis on snow. Side to side. Push with long, sharp poles. Triceps whine, shins scream, thighs grumble. The brain, the old monkey mind, scolds: *You're going to kill us.*

At first my skis were too fast. I slipped and caught an edge in the snow but kept pushing with my poles, alternating skis, shifting weight to each leg. As my skis cooled to snow temperature, I began to glide. Yes. Glide. My eyes watered and my nose dripped. No matter. Between fear and ache, exhilaration. I remembered the lessons I had taken, the advice of my young coaches. Eyes, nose, and toes. Line them up. Weight on one side, shift to the other. Move your hips as you shift weight side to side—sexy skiing.

The trail was fast, my wax perfect. I was skimming the snow, panting, heart pounding, flowing side to side, observing the tracks left by the travelers ahead of me: skiers, bikers, walkers. How good it felt to be alive.

Four young skiers had built a snow jump at the bottom of a hill off the main trail. They flew down the slope, launched into the air, and somehow landed upright, laughing. I envied their courage, the confidence their bodies would respond exactly as they wanted.

I glided past them, past the years and fears, to that winter of so much snow, to that small girl venturing into the wonders of the big North. Snow tunnels, angels, moose at the windows. Skating with my dad, his hand in mine, sharing a moment of grace, rhythm, and love.

Acknowledgments

The City of Anchorage sits on the traditional homeland of the Eklutna Dena'ina people. I wish to acknowledge and respect the land, culture and language of the Dena'ina people, who thrived in this land long before my family and previous generations of settlers arrived.

I am thankful for the support of my husband Jim Thiele during the many years it took to bring this book to fruition. He had faith in me even when I doubted I could finish this project.

Thanks also to my daughter, Elisha, son-in-law Chad, and grandchildren Cason and Carly for their grace in accepting my portrayals of them throughout this book, and to my sisters Patty and Teri for allowing me to tell one version of our family's story.

I also wish to thank early readers of this manuscript, who convinced me that there was a thread worth following in the original collection of essays, many of which became the chapters in this final form. I could not have gone forward without the honest feedback of Trish Joyner, Ellen Nash, Kathy Kline, and Sherri Douglas, as well as the steadfast encouragement and honest critiques from the members of my writing group, Barbara Hood, Lynn Haltquist, and Thomas Pease.

Special thanks to Deb Vanasse, author, mentor, teacher, editor, and unwavering advocate in my path to publication. As the co-founder, with Andromeda Romano-Lax, of 49 Writers, I would not have been able to take advantage of the many opportunities provided by the amazing community of Alaskan writers without your support.

I am grateful to the many authors and teachers who believed in my potential and urged me to take risks as a writer, including Peggy Shumaker, former writer laureate of Alaska; Craig Childs, author and faculty member at Orion Nature Writers Workshop; Bill Sherwonit, Alaskan nature writer and advocate of Alaska's wild lands and animals; and the late Sherry Simpson, of the University of Alaska Creative Writing Program, who helped me learn to see the northern landscape and translate my vision into words. I would like to especially honor the late Frank Soos, author, mentor, and extraordinary teacher, who read my early essays and suggested that I had a collection worth sharing with a broader audience.

Thanks to the members of my women's hiking group, the WADs, (you know who you are) for helping me do what I did not know I could do, and to the many friends and family members who believed I could reach the finish line.

I especially want to thank my parents, Paul and Dorothy, for having the courage to leave behind all that was familiar to them and take a chance on Alaska.

Lastly, I could not have written this book without the extraordinary vision and craftsmanship of Michael Charney, of Riddle Brook Publishing. I am grateful for his belief in my story, and his ability to help me find the threads to pull these many fragments into a coherent whole. I could not have succeeded without him.

Thanks also to the journals, anthologies, and magazines that previously published work contained here in previous forms, including, *Cirque, A Literary Journal of the North Pacific Rim*; *Ravensperch*; *Under the Gum Tree*; *Alaska Magazine*; *Hippocampus*; *Anchorage Remembers: A Century of Tales*; *Burrow Press Review*; *Under the Sun*; *Deep Waters*; *The Delmarva Review*; *Persimmon Tree*; and *Pilgrimage.*

About the Author

Susan Pope's writing has been shaped by growing up in the wide and wild landscape of Alaska. Her stories reveal the tension between a desire for intimate ties to home and community, and a longing to flee to faraway places.

With humor, humility, and courage she explores topics as diverse as mountain climbing, motherhood, the secrets of a lost diary, a crumbling family legacy, the disappointments of grandparenthood, and a fear of drowning. Her settings range from her backyard bike trails to the Kalahari desert.

Susan Pope's work has appeared in *Pilgrimage*, *Under the Sun*, *The Southeast Review Online*, *Cirque: A Literary Journal of the Pacific Rim*, *Crosscurrents North: Alaskans on the Environment*, *Hippocampus*, *Under the Gum Tree*, *Burrow Press Review*, *BioStories*, *Writers' Workshop Review*, *Alaska Magazine*, *Bluestem*, and *Burningword Literary Review*, among others. Her writing reflects intimate connections to home and family in Alaska as well as a restless pursuit of faraway places. She writes from her home in Anchorage, Alaska.

www.ingramcontent.com/pod-product-compliance
Lightning Source LLC
Chambersburg PA
CBHW022047020426
42335CB00012B/585

* 9 7 9 8 9 8 5 9 4 1 3 6 4 *